Dare to Live Without Limits

by
Bryan Golden

Power Point Press
Beekman, New York

The author may be contacted at info@BryanGolden.com. Web site: www.BryanGolden.com

Bryan writes a column, *Dare to Live Without Limits,* that is carried by various publications and is distributed throughout the country. Please contact Bryan to add his popular and widely read column to your publication.

Bryan is available to give a presentation to your group or meeting or for consultation.

This book is ideal for distribution throughout corporations and organizations. Volume discounts are available. Contact the author for details.

ISBN 0-9753688-0-X
Library of Congress Control Number: 2004106182

Cover photography by Sally Delmerico
Cover design by Kevin Masters
Edited by Kristine Horend and Sally Delmerico

Dedication

This book is dedicated to my parents, Sam and Rachelle, and the love of my life, Sally. It is because of the love and support of these very special people that this book was possible.

Contents

Introduction

This exceptional book shows you many ways to take positive control of and enrich your life. You will learn techniques and see examples of how others have used simple, yet time tested, methods to triumph over adversity, stress, and misfortune to stay sane in an insane world. The concepts presented within enable you to break through those limitations preventing you from achieving your goals and realizing your dreams.

This book is based on the popular and widely read *Dare to Live Without Limits* newspaper column. Each topic is expanded upon with many how-to examples that were not included in the newspaper column due to space limitations.

All of the principles, concepts, and strategies presented within are proven and effective. They have been successfully utilized throughout history by people from every walk of life.

Reading this book is only the first step. Sincere and consistent application of this information can enrich your life beyond measure. All of us have developed many unproductive thinking habits throughout our lives. Changing these habits does not happen overnight.

1

BRYAN GOLDEN

Developing new ways of thinking and acting requires constant repetition.

I can personally attest to the fact that all of the information presented here works. I have applied each concept to my life and experienced the wonderful effects they produce. I make no claims as to how quickly things will work for you. But the more effort and energy you invest in yourself, the faster any changes will occur. Be patient, have faith and never, ever give up.

This book is designed to be easy to read and fits into any hectic lifestyle. Each chapter is self-contained and can be read in any order. The chapters are intentionally short so that they may be read quickly.

For maximum effectiveness, read and re-read each chapter. Each time you do so, you will discover something you may have missed before. Through repetition you are re-training your mind to think without limits.

Society in general tends to be negative. As positive as you may be, you need to recharge your attitude on a regular basis. Even though staying positive, like staying in shape, requires constant effort, the rewards are phenomenal. This book is your recharger.

If you want to really reinforce this material, explain and share it with others. Teaching and sharing is one of the most effective ways of learning. Also, by helping others to grow, you can't help growing yourself.

Remember that as you apply the material presented, you are in the company of the multitude of people who have

2

utilized these very same concepts to enrich their lives throughout the history of mankind.

1. The Power Within

Living without limits. Living your life to the fullest. Living with happiness. Living your dreams. Living free from fear and worry. You have the power to live your life any way you want. Your mind has awesome, untapped power that you can harness to direct, improve, and enrich your life.

Why doesn't everyone utilize their mind to the fullest? There are several reasons. People are unaware of the power that they possess. People don't believe they have the potential that they do. People don't know how to utilize their potential.

You will never be as young as you are today. Life is not a practice run. So squeeze the most out of every day. Whatever has happened to you in the past is over. Don't allow your past to pollute your future. All that matters is what you do today.

To live life your way, you have access to the most powerful tool ever known. This marvelous tool is your mind. It can be your ally or your enemy – the choice is yours.

To harness your mind's virtually unlimited power you must regularly feed it the right thoughts. Positive or negative, your mind digests and processes whatever you feed it. Only you can control your mental diet.

You can direct your mind to bring you the life that you really want. You don't have to settle or suffer. Only thoughts and attitudes differentiate success from failure. There are many definitions of success, but there is only one definition of failure: giving up. Winners never quit and quitters never win.

Everyone has problems and every problem has a solution. Problems are not something to be feared. They provide an opportunity to learn and grow. With every adversity there is an equivalent or greater opportunity. Successful people utilize their problems as stepping stones to reach their goals. Others use their problems as excuses to justify where they are and why they can't do more.

There's no escaping the law of cause and effect. If you do what you've always done, you'll continue to get what you've always gotten. To have different results you must take different action. Success is only possible by reaching out and extending into the unknown.

Don't fear failure. The concept of failure is learned; we are not born with it. Success is simply getting up one more time than you fall down. You haven't failed unless you stop getting up. To double your rate of success, double your failure rate.

Throughout life, we are told what we can't do. We hear "no" more than we hear "yes". To achieve success, we must unlearn the concept of failure. Those who succeed have purged their vocabularies of all negative concepts such as "failure", "won't work" and "can't do."

Consider the following examples:

• The Apple microcomputer was turned down by both Hewlett-Packard and Atari, but had first year sales of $2.5 million.

• In his first year in the automobile business, Henry Ford went bankrupt. Two years later, his second company also failed. His third corporation has done rather well, however.

• Dr. Seuss's first children's book was rejected by 23 publishers; the 24th publisher sold six million copies of it.

• Howard Hughes Sr. was forced to abandon his first oil well because he couldn't drill through the hard rock. He then founded Hughes Tool Co. and invented a rock drill that became the foundation for the family fortune.

• R.H. Macy went broke with his first three dry-goods stores.

• After Paul Galvin's storage-battery business failed for the second time in 1928, he borrowed $750, bought back part of it and went into business again as Motorola.

These are just a few examples of what the mind can accomplish. The people in these examples didn't possess anything that isn't available to you. You have unlimited potential. Whether you realize it is up to you. Your only limitations are the ones you impose upon yourself.

The application of these principles will touch and improve every aspect of your life. You can live without limits!

2. The Basic Principles: An Overview

There are specific principles that can be utilized to reach your fullest potential. This chapter provides an overview while the following ones go into more detail. All of these principles are proven and time tested. They work reliably if implemented faithfully and consistently.

A change in action precedes a change in results. Only you can alter those aspects of your life you are not happy with. You can not blame anyone else for your situation. You can not depend on anyone else to alter your circumstances. What happens in your life is your choice.

These concepts, although simple and straightforward, can seem difficult to carry out. Why? Because their application requires us to think and act in a manner different from what we are used to. Altering entrenched patterns of thought and action isn't easy. Improvements will not happen overnight. As you start to modify your habits you will notice definite results. Don't get discouraged or frustrated. Countless others have achieved a rich and rewarding life through the application of these principles. You can to!

All of the following principles are interrelated. For the best results they should be applied simultaneously.

- You are what you think about
- Set goals
- Plan how to reach your goals
- All we have is today
- Never ever give up
- Education never ends
- Control your own emotions
- Guard your time
- Have an attitude of gratitude
- What you project you receive

1. You are what you think about

Your attitude and what you think determines who you are. How you think is the only thing differentiating you from others. Twenty-four hours a day your mind operates to figure out ways which will bring your thoughts to reality. Positive thoughts or negative, your mind doesn't discriminate. Like a freshly plowed field, your mind grows whatever seeds of thought you plant.

Only you can select the seeds of thought which are planted. The *only* thing you have absolute control over is your attitude and thoughts. Always be positive and visualize success. Act the way you want to be. If you think you can do something you are right. If you think you can't do something, you are also right. The choice is yours.

2. Set goals

What do you want from life? You don't need to project years into the future. You need to determine what you want now. It doesn't matter what your goals are so long as they are *your* goals and don't involve hurting others. Write down your goals and read them every day. Goals give you a definiteness of purpose and are the map to your desired destination.

If you don't know what you want, spend time analyzing yourself to determine what you like and don't like. Make two lists. One will contain everything you want from life, the other what you don't want. Develop these lists without any restrictions.

List everything, even if you think it seems unrealistic. These lists will enable you to set immediate goals. Without goals, you have no direction or destination and are like a rudderless ship on the ocean, much more likely to run aground than arrive safely in port.

3. Plan how to reach your goals

Determine what steps are necessary to reach your goals. Goals can seem overwhelming and unreachable if not broken down into a series of small, manageable steps. If you don't know what steps to take, look to those who are where you want to be. How did they start and what path did they take?

This information can be found through personal contact, newspaper articles, magazine stories, and books. Every goal is reachable by taking the appropriate steps and never giving up. Each journey starts at the beginning. Of all the steps, the most important is the first. Consistently taking one step after another will inevitably bring you to your goal.

It doesn't matter how long it takes since the time will go by regardless of whether or not you are pursuing your goals. Don't suffer from paralysis by analysis. Get started now, today!

4. All we have is today

The past can easily distract and affect you. Regardless of what you feel you should have, would have, or could have done differently, you can never go back in time to change anything. Yesterday is gone forever. If you dwell on the past your positive energy and motivation will be compromised.

Don't allow your past to pollute your present. Learn from your past, don't repeat it. Every day is a fresh start. The only direction you can go is forward. If you want to do something, start today. Today will become tomorrow's yesterday. Act now so that tomorrow you don't regret what you didn't do today.

5. Never ever give up

Nothing is possible without persistence. You never know around which corner or beyond which obstacle your success lies. So why would you ever give up? There is no such thing as failure. People think they have failed because they don't get up after falling down.

Things may not work out as quickly as you would like. So what. Time goes by anyway. What difference does it make how long it takes to reach your goal? If it's what you want, get started, keep going and don't stop. Focus your energy and always keep your goals in sight. Everything worthwhile takes effort.

You will hear that it's not easy to succeed. This is true. But it's not any easier to live a life of unfulfilled goals. Ironically it takes more effort to endure a life of unrealized potential than to work toward success. So, since living life takes effort, no matter what you do, why not strive for success?

6. Education never ends

Never stop learning. Education is a lifetime endeavor. Formal schooling is the least significant part of your education. Keep your mind open to learn new things every day.

Every person you come into contact with has something to teach you. It doesn't matter what someone else's educational level, social status, or age is. Learn from those you like and admire as well as from those you don't care for.

Each situation you experience has something to teach you. When things work out as planned, you can learn. When things don't work out as expected, you can learn. Actually, you can learn more when things don't work than when they do.

In order to learn, your mind must be open and receptive. There must be room for new ideas. If a water glass is full, you can't add more water. If you feel that you know everything, your mind is full and has no room for new ideas.

7. Control your own emotions

Don't allow others to control your emotions. Although you can't control your environment you can control your reaction to it. It doesn't matter what other people say, think, or do. What does matter is what you say, think, and do. Often those closest to you, family and friends, will be the most critical and judgmental of your goals and plans.

Everyone who has ever accomplished anything has at some point been laughed at and criticized. Every technological and societal development that benefits us today was only possible because their innovators kept to their path despite the condemnation of others. You can't control other people's opinions and actions but you can control your response.

If you want to attain other people's goals then follow their advice. If you want to reach your own goals, follow your own path. It's not easy, but it's worth it!

8. Guard your time

Twenty-four hours a day is all the time any person has. There is a special bank account where 86,400 new seconds are deposited for you every day. You choose how to spend your daily balance. Each day any unused or wasted balance is zeroed out and lost forever, nothing carries forward.

Granted, not all of your time is discretionary. You may be spending time at a job you don't like. But how is the rest of each day spent? Is your free time spent with people who share your positive attitude and encourage you or with people who are negative and discouraging?

Do you spend your free time working towards your goals? Every second that goes by is gone forever; it's your choice how to use it. Your time is one of your most precious commodities. Guard your time and don't allow negative people or activities to steal it.

9. Have an attitude of gratitude

Be thankful for and appreciate all that you have, whatever your circumstances may be. Take nothing for granted. Don't compare your life to others. Never be resentful or bitter about what you feel you don't have.

Bitterness is a poison. It will erode your mental and physical health. Bitterness will prohibit you from accomplishing your goals. No matter how bad you think your predicament is, people throughout history have endured hardships and overcome adversities that are unimaginable.

Don't blow your situation out of proportion. Focus on the abundance in your life. Every problem has a solution. Appreciate what you have and you will always have more than you need. If you constantly want more you will never have enough.

Strive to develop your character into the person that you want to be. Character will serve you for a lifetime and can never be lost or taken away. What you have doesn't determine who you are; who you are determines what you have.

10. What you project you receive

You are a magnet. Your attitude and actions determine what you attract. A good attitude and good actions attract

13

BRYAN GOLDEN

good people and situations and vice versa. You can get everything you want in your life by helping other people get what they want.

Don't give with the expectation of what you will get in return. If rewards are your motivation, they will elude you. Only by giving without the expectation of receiving will rewards follow.

Anyone can smile and laugh when things are going well. But you must learn to smile and laugh when life seems to be at a low point. Only then will you be able to bounce back from adversity and continue the journey towards your goals.

If you are waiting for your situation to improve before your attitude improves, you will be waiting a very long time. Whatever you situation, attitude always precedes results. Whatever your circumstances are, you can improve them. No one can stop you. Only you can stop yourself.

Start today to act as if you already are where you want to be. Do whatever you can to help others.

3. You Are What You Think About

You have complete control over your thoughts. Thought patterns develop over a lifetime and are a result of the influences of schooling, parents, friends, relatives, TV, movies, etc. Many of the examples you are exposed to, either real or fictional, portray a type of thinking that is the antithesis of possibility thinking.

Unfortunately, most of the guidance received about how to think is negative. More effort is spent teaching what you can't do rather than what you can. Whatever your thinking is now, you can learn to alter it. Seek out and study the thinking of successful people.

Why reinvent the wheel? There are numerous examples of people who have achieved whatever it is that you want to do. Take a look around you. There are people you know, people you know about, people in the news, and historical figures who have harnessed and directed their thoughts to actualize their dreams.

Mark Allen, a six-time ironman triathlon champion, started by studying the techniques of previous winners. He wanted to know how they trained and prepared themselves. Allen then incorporated their successful techniques into his own practice sessions.

Another powerful mental tool that Allen utilized was visualization. Allen visualized his performance of the next event before sleeping. Athletes have found that visualizing successful accomplishment can be as effective as the actual physical training.

An American prisoner of war in Vietnam visualized playing golf every day to help endure the hardships of captivity. After being released, his golf skills had markedly improved even though he hadn't physically played in years.

Visualization is one of the most powerful techniques you can employ to change your thinking. Through visualization, you direct the desired outcome in your mind. In your mind you can overcome any obstacle and solve any problem. You may rehearse a situation over and over anytime and anywhere.

Visualization affords you all the benefits of repetitive practice without any of the pitfalls. Through visualization you avoid physical injury, ridicule, embarrassment, financial hardship, and perceived failure. Visualization enables your mind to experience perfect performance.

In actuality your mind doesn't differentiate between real practice and visualized practice. When you first actually attempt to perform the activity you visualized, the successful scenario is so engrained it governs the way you perform.

The activities that lend themselves to visualization are virtually endless. Job interviews, sales presentations, public speaking, sports, interacting with difficult people, asking for a raise, and accomplishing goals are just some examples.

You must condition your mind to be impervious to negative criticism. Rather than wanting to join you on your goal-achieving quest, most people would instead prefer you to fail. Other people will be jealous. There's nothing you can do to control their thoughts.

The first modern rocket scientist, Robert Goddard, a physics professor, had his research denounced by the press. In 1920, a newspaper editorial stated that Goddard "seems to lack the knowledge ladled out daily in high schools."

Amid condemnation and with little support from fellow scientists, Goddard became a leading pioneer of the space era. He achieved success by focusing on reaching his goals instead of what people thought of his research.

Develop a belief in your goals and the path you choose to achieve them. It takes a lot of practice to free yourself from what other people say, think, or do. You must overcome a strong societal outlook that other people's opinion of you is important.

The discoverer of the Titanic wreck, Robert Ballard, tried unsuccessfully for 12 years to obtain financing needed for his search. Additionally, hunting for the Titanic was considered folly by several fellow scientists. Yet, with an unshakable belief in himself and his goals, he overcame all obstacles and found the wreckage in 1985.

The type of thinking that all successful people possess is available to you. You can opt to pattern your thinking after those who have achieved success, often despite overwhelming odds.

Changing your thinking requires effort. Many people who are close to you won't understand or support your endeavors. If you are laughed at and criticized, this is good. It means that you are experiencing the same reaction as some of the greatest minds in history and are in the best of company.

4. Perception is Reality

How do you experience your world? Is your glass half full or half empty? Do you observe the worst in a situation or the best? Do you justify identifying only negatives by claiming you are being realistic?

Two people can experience the exact same event and yet have radically different perceptions. Some people escape unscathed regardless of what befalls them. Others are problem magnets. Why?

A person's perception defines their reality. Perception is controlled by attitude. You control your attitude. Therefore you control your reality. Since you have the ability to control your reality, wouldn't you want to make your reality as ideal as possible?

Yet many people allow their attitude to taint their reality. For every problem do you see a solution or do you find a problem in every situation? Your link to the world is through your senses. They feed a stream of raw, unfiltered information into your brain. Perception is your interpretation of this information.

The orientation of your perception has a cascading effect. Often, it's a self-fulfilling prophecy. What you anticipate frequently happens. You attract what you think about. This phenomenon may not be explainable scientifically, but it exists and functions consistently.

People advertise negative perception through their comments. "I'm an accident waiting to happen." "I can never make anything work." "No one ever understands me." "I always get into arguments." "People get the wrong impression of me."

It's just as easy to identify those with a positive perception. "Don't worry, we'll get through this." "There's always a solution." "It's a blessing in disguise." "There's no reason to get upset, this is just a learning experience."

Why do different people have radically diverse perceptions? Perceptual development is influenced by many factors. Examples set by parents have a substantial impact. Additionally the influence of friends, schools, and role models make a major impression. A person's own experiences also shape their perception.

There is an experience-perception cycle. Positive experiences lead to positive perceptions while negative experiences lead to negative perceptions. Your perceptions become engrained as they are reinforced experientially. If you are caught in a positive cycle, you're in good shape. When you are in a negative one, you must break out.

A negative perception impedes your progress, while a positive one benefits you. Regardless of the circumstances you may encounter, a positive perception enables you to uncover the most beneficial ways to respond.

Your perception influences the type of situations and people you attract. Like attracts like. A positive perception attracts beneficial situations and people. Through a positive perception you will discover solutions to life's challenges.

Consider this example. You have an important presentation. Not wanting to be late, you leave 45 minutes early. On your way, you lose a half-hour in a traffic jam. As traffic starts to move you get a flat tire.

The negative perception approach:

You become stressed and frantic. Rushing to change the tire, you rip your shirt and get grease on your clothes. You wind up being 10 minutes late. You charge into the meeting half crazed and disheveled. Your presentation is awful because you can't focus on it.

The positive perception approach:

You know everything will be OK. You've overcome more challenging problems than a flat tire. You remain relaxed and change the tire without getting dirty. Although you arrive at the meeting 10 minutes late, you stride in with renewed confidence. Your presentation is fantastic and no one cared you were delayed.

To develop a positive perception, look at every situation as containing a gift or hidden treasure. Uncovering the treasure is possible only through a belief in its existence. You are capable of locating it. Don't stop looking until it's discovered. The treasure is there and you will find it. Once a situation exists you may as well turn it to your advantage. To do otherwise doesn't benefit anyone and is a complete waste.

5. Throw Out the Garbage

What would happen to your home if you never took out the garbage? How long would it be before the trash forced you out? Or how would you feel if someone came into your home carrying a pail of their refuse and dumped it in the middle of your brand new living room carpet?

Your home would become completely uninhabitable long before it filled up with garbage. When cleaning your home, you don't throw out everything. Discretion is used to discard the waste while keeping your valuables.

Bad thoughts, negative attitudes, clinging to the past, and bad experiences are garbage in your mind. Many people hoard their mental trash. Subsequently, their mental landfill swells over the years limiting their progress.

The mind functions like a video camera. Everything is caught on mental tape; what you do, what happens to you, what you say, and what you hear. Good experiences and bad are captured, successes and failures are recorded.

Your mind is the camera, but you are the omnipotent director. You have sole discretion as to which scenes are kept, which are edited, and which are replaced. Whether or not you exercise your directorial power is your choice.

So how do you throw out mental trash? The concept is simple but its application takes practice. Be a proactive director. When creating a movie, a director will discard any scene that doesn't contribute to the quality of the film. If a scene can't be salvaged through editing, it's removed.

When a movie is made, more film will be eliminated and wind up on the cutting room floor than will make it into the final product that you see on the screen. Similarly, there are fewer mental images worth keeping compared to those that should be discarded.

Review each major scene stored in your mind. Keep those that contribute positively to your well being. Get rid of the others. Ironically, it's common for many people to do just the opposite. They constantly replay all of the negative scenes. They relive, and dwell in, those memories that were unpleasant, caused pain, or were frustrating.

Whatever mental images you recall and replay evoke the same emotions you felt when they were first recorded. There is no differentiation between the feelings experienced during the original event and those generated from the replay. When you bring the negative memories to the forefront, the good and positive memories are pushed to the background and sometimes forgotten altogether.

Your mind doesn't discriminate when you replay your mental video. Any scene you request will be faithfully rerun. As the director, you have control over what's played, when, and how often. You want to retain and replay those memories that make you feel good. Before discarding the garbage, pick through it and salvage that which is valuable. Regardless of how bad the memory, there was a lesson learned or insight gained. Separate and save these jewels.

Memories can't be forgotten, they have to be replaced. It's impossible to not think of something. If I say to you "don't think about ice cream," what will you think about? Ice cream. So to get rid of your mental garbage you have to displace it with the valuable stuff. Concentration on good and positive thoughts causes the other memories to fade away. Pack your mind so full of valuable thoughts that the garbage is forced out.

6. Set Goals

Why is it important to set goals? Goals give your life a specific direction enabling you to keep on course. Goals make your path one of design rather than happenstance.

Karl Mladen Sekulovich, a 21-year-old son of Serbian immigrants, was determined to not spend his life working in the steel mills in Gary, Indiana as were his contemporaries. In 1934, Karl took his life savings of $340 and went to Chicago to study acting.

Driven by his goals, the budding actor, who would become known as Karl Malden, used $300 to pay for the first semester of acting school. He then went on to win a full scholarship for the entire three-year program.

Explorer Ferdinand Magellan's goal was to find a passage connecting the Atlantic and Pacific oceans. In 1520, while sailing through horrendous weather, the crew doubted Magellan's course and urged him to abort the trip. Perseverance and an unshakable belief in his goals enabled him to discover the passage.

Maurice Ashley, the first African-American to hold the highest ranking in chess, international grandmaster, loved chess as a teenager. He practiced and learned as much as possible and decided that becoming a grandmaster would be his goal in life.

Imagine your car's windshield painted black. What are your chances of staying on the road without crashing? Your life without goals is like driving your car without seeing the road. Goals are targets that you aim for.

How do you determine your goals? You must first decide where you want to go in life. Goals can be modified, changed, or added to at any time, so don't be afraid that setting them will restrict you.

Your goals must be your own. Others will try to influence you, but you can't achieve their goals. If goals aren't yours, attaining them won't bring you satisfaction or happiness.

Setting goals requires a thorough self-analysis. Start by determining what you want and don't want. Make two lists as if you had no limitations. The first list details all of your desires. The second list contains those things that don't appeal to you. On the list of what you want rank the entries in order of importance to you. The most important entries should be considered major goals.

Don't worry about what other people may think about your lists. These are your private compilations and they don't have to be shown or discussed with anyone. Once you have made these lists, compare them to your current situation. If you find you are doing things you don't want to do, you may feel frustrated and dissatisfied.

You will never be satisfied achieving someone else's goals. There are too many examples of people who have achieved goals set by parents, siblings, spouses, or friends. These people are typically unhappy, frustrated, and unfulfilled.

If you subvert your goals to conform to other people's opinions, you shortchange yourself. It's tempting to try to make others understand and accept your goals, but they don't have to. What's important is that you are comfortable and happy with your goals.

Time goes by too fast to spend it being miserable. We learn to justify our current existence even if we are not happy with it. You can realize your dreams. Whatever your goals may be, someone else has already achieved them. If someone else can do it, you can do it too.

If you're not satisfied with your current direction or circumstances, alter them. It's never too late or too early to set goals and begin to transform your life. If you don't take action, nothing will change.

7. Plan to Reach Your Goals

Goals are your destination. Your plan is the map. Without a plan, goals are only a dream. A plan will keep you on track and enable you to realize your dreams. Persistence is the fuel that will drive you to attain your goals. Many attempts may be required, possibly altering plans along the way, before you reach your destination.

Pursuing your goals is like digging in a gold mine. You know the gold is there. If you dig long enough and deep enough, in the right location, you will find it. But if you stop, even if you are only an inch away from riches, the results are exactly the same as if you never started.

Arthur Blank and Bernie Marcus, lost their jobs running Handy Dan Home Centers in 1978. They saw as opportunity what most would consider bad luck. Both knew the hardware business and sought to apply their experience to create something new. After extensive research, they formulated their goals and stayed focused on them. In 1979, they started the Home Depot chain.

How do you begin formulating a plan to reach your goals? To determine how to get somewhere, ask someone who has already gone where you want to go. If you want to learn how to fly, talk to a Chuck Yeager. To learn how to invest, talk to a Warren Buffet. The best guides are those who have already successfully traveled the route you want to take.

Everyone will have an opinion as to what you should do. Only listen to those who are where you want to be. The most common mistake is taking advice from the wrong people. Don't waste time reinventing the wheel. Experience may be a good teacher, but someone else's experience is the best teacher.

It takes a lot of effort and research to devise a plan. Doing the research is like building a foundation. The deeper the foundation, the taller the building that can be built. Skimp on the foundation and the entire structure it supports will be shaky.

In 1873 a 14-year-old boy arrived from Germany and settled in Detroit. Needing a job quickly, he became a butcher boy. Moving to Chicago three years later, he decided the meat business had a future there. He knew that to understand a business he had to have first hand experience in each part of it.

He continued his apprenticeship eventually becoming a stockyard assistant and then a retail meat salesman. He saw an opportunity to sell German style meats to the numerous German immigrants in Chicago. In 1883, the now 24-year-old Oscar F. Mayer, who never attended high school, founded his meat business.

You must have the attitude that you will reach your goals and will do whatever it takes to do so (as long as it's ethical and doesn't harm others.) Failure is not an option. If one plan doesn't work, you will formulate another one. You will persist until your goals are achieved.

Reaching your goals can seem overwhelming without a plan comprised of a series of achievable steps. A journey always starts with the first step. It's easy to slip into the trap of procrastinating about starting. But start you must. Don't get caught lamenting "if only I had started before."

Write your plan down and read it daily. Make several copies and post them around your home. Take one with you to work. When you regularly review your plan, you imbed it into your conscious and subconscious thoughts.

8. An Eight Step Plan to Reach Your Goals

Step 1. Compile a list of people who are where you want to be or have accomplished what you want to do. This list can include anybody. If you can't think of anyone, do some research. The internet is a wonderful tool for this. These people are an important resource because they have lots of valuable experience you can learn from.

Step 2. Contact any people on the list you know personally. Explain your goals and ask how they achieved theirs. Most people will be flattered and happy to speak with you. Be generous; offer to do something for them in return for their time. For people on your list that you don't know, read everything written about or by them. Search for magazine or newspaper articles or books. If contact information is available, write them explaining your goals and asking if they could give you any advice or suggestions.

You want to find out how each person got started, what path they took, what obstacles were encountered, and how they overcame them. If they were starting over again, what would they do differently?

Step 3. Once you have gathered as much information as possible, start to develop your own customized plan. List everything you'll require to reach your goal. Take inventory of what you currently have and identify what you'll need.

Whatever you require is obtainable. Do you need more education, partners, money, motivation, time, or a different location? Everyone has problems and every problem has one or more solutions. Successful people focus on solutions, not problems.

If you lack expertise you can go to school, read books, apprentice, or hire an expert. If you need money you can find ways to increase your income, save more, borrow, or find investors. If you lack time you can find more by eliminating non-productive activities or by bringing in a partner.

Step 4. Write out a major plan of action. It should be broad, not detailed, listing the major steps needed to reach your goals.

For example, if you wanted to open your own restaurant the major steps might be: learn the restaurant business, decide whether to buy a business or start a new one, pick a location, determine your price range, obtain funding, buy or start the business.

Step 5. Break down each major step into smaller sub-steps. With the above illustration, how would you learn the restaurant business? Will you go to school or apprentice by working in a restaurant? Perhaps you want to bring in a partner who has this knowledge.

Step 6. Create a plan of action to achieve each sub-step. Be as detailed as possible and have a specific timetable. For example, if you decide to go to school, what school, how you will pay for it, when you will start, how long it will take, will you attend full or part time.

If you will apprentice, where and for how long. If you will use a partner, do you know someone, or if not, how will you find someone? The sub-steps should be small enough so that they can be readily accomplished and aren't intimidating.

Step 7. Begin, take the first step. At this point you should have a very detailed road map of how you plan to achieve your goals. Consider your plans adjustable and never hesitate to make changes as you progress, learn, and grow.

Step 8. Continue, step by step until you realize your goals. Set a timetable for your progress. Work on each step on a regular and consistent basis. Consistency is essential. If you work on your plan in fits and spurts, progress will be tedious if it's made at all. You must make time to work on your plan. You can't work on it only when you manage to fit it into your schedule and expect to make meaningful progress. Set up a schedule and keep to it without fail. Even if you can only work on your plan for one hour a week, do so.

Every journey, regardless of the length, is completed by taking one step after another. To reach your destination you must persist until the last step has been taken. There is no secret. There is no magic.

9. The Secrets of Achievement

Achieving whatever you want is possible by incorporating the following "secrets" into your daily schedule. Consistency is key. To enjoy positive results, you need to make these secrets a way of life. All of the secrets are equally important. You can't pick and choose. These secrets are not sequential steps. They have to be applied simultaneously.

If you're not used to integrating these concepts into your life, you may feel awkward at first. Your comfort level will grow as you repeatedly apply them. Eventually, they will become second nature and you will wonder why everyone doesn't use them. Go ahead and indulge yourself. Overdosing isn't possible and there are no negative side effects. Only good things will result.

S: Sense of purpose. You need goals, a clear vision of what you want, and an understanding of your destination. Live with intention. A definite sense of purpose is your treasure map. Without it, you are like a cork floating on the ocean; the wind, waves, currents, and tides determining your direction. When distractions arise, a sense of purpose keeps you on track.

E: Excellence. Be the best you can at everything you do. If you don't commit to, and demand excellence, you broadcast that you accept mediocrity. Acceptance of mediocrity demonstrates a lack of concern. If you don't care, how can you expect anyone else to? First rate attracts first rate. Excellence places you far ahead of the crowd.

C: Contribution. Doing for others, service and giving. You can have anything in life you want by helping enough other people get what they want. Rewards are a result, not a goal. They are proportional to how much you are willing to give. But only if you give without the expectation of receiving. All of your actions will come full circle, but there's no way to know when, where, or how.

R: Responsibility. Take 100% responsibility for your life. Don't blame others. Doing so dooms you to a life of frustration and disappointment. Success or failure, everyone is self-made. You are responsible for where you are today. If you don't like your situation, change it.

E: Effort. There is no shortcut or substitute for focus and hard work. Work smart and hard. Anything worthwhile takes effort. Exceed what is expected. In order for an airplane to take off, all engines must be set to full throttle. Once airborne, the engines are throttled back for level flight. Power has to be increased in response to turbulence or to gain more altitude. Life works the same way. All endeavors require 110% effort to get them off the ground. Once momentum builds, you can throttle back and enjoy the results of your efforts.

T: Time management. Use discretion in how you spend your time. Each day has only 24 hours. Set priorities. Address the most important items first. Ignore tasks that don't have negative repercussions if they go undone. Say no to those people and activities that distract you from your objectives. Reserve your time for those actions that bring you closer to your goals. Use time, don't waste it.

S: Stay with it. Persist and persevere. Never, ever give up. You won't accomplish anything without resolve. No matter how hopeless or impossible a situation may seem, persistence gives you have the ability to triumph. There is nothing more powerful than pure, dogged tenacity. Determination can even compensate for other areas that may be lacking such as education, experience, or finances.

These secrets of achievement can be utilized by anyone, at anytime. It doesn't matter what has happened in the past. Start applying and enjoying all of these secrets today.

10. Never Ever Give Up

Persistence is the foundation of success. Although there are many ways to describe success, there is only one definition of failure – giving up. Whatever your meaning of success, you will only achieve it through persistence.

"Nothing in the world can take the place of persistence.
Talent will not; nothing is more common than unsuccessful men with talent.
Genius will not; unrewarded genius is almost a proverb.
Education will not; the world is full of educated derelicts.
Persistence and determination alone are omnipotent."
Calvin Coolidge

Babe Ruth had more strike outs than anyone else in history. When asked about the key to his success he said, "I just keep swinging." Everyone who achieves success does so because they keep swinging. They never stop. If something doesn't work as planned, they keep going.

In the mid 1960's, Martin Cooper, an electrical engineer at Motorola, had a vision of a phone that could be carried around and powered by a battery. His concept was scoffed at by many of his fellow engineers. After 15 years in development, Motorola brought the cellular phone to market.

37

In 1864, he was born the son of slaves on a Missouri plantation. He grew up not knowing his parents. With persistence and determination he put himself through college. To combat the racism he encountered, he excelled in everything he did. George Washington Carver became one of our nation's leading scientists and revolutionized agriculture.

At 205 pounds and standing 5'10" tall he was below average size for a pro football player. To build his strength and endurance he ran up steep hills while playing high school football. As a professional player he ran up an 80-yard hill, set at a 45-degree angle, 25 times a day. Determined to be the best he could be, he watched films of opponents until he could predict their moves. Football Hall of Famer, Walter Payton tied or beat seven NFL records during his 13-season career.

You are born without the concept of failure. How did you learn to walk? The first time you tried you immediately fell. But since you didn't know you couldn't succeed you immediately tried again. And again you fell down. But you never gave up. Hundreds of times you repeated this process until you learned to walk.

Persistence is getting up one more time than you fall down. Unfortunately, you are taught to give up and fail. How many times have you heard one or more of the following?

"Why bother, you'll never be able to do that – it'll never work."
"Don't rock the boat, just do what you're supposed to do."
"Why take chances?"

"You'll never amount to anything."
"Stop dreaming -- come back to reality."
"Why don't you give up already?"
"I tried that already, it doesn't work."

If you had believed any of the above when you were learning to walk, you'd still be crawling! You didn't listen to bad advice then so why listen to it now?

When you feel like giving up, you must keep going. Only by continuing, when most others won't, will you achieve your goals. Don't join the ranks of those who have given up just around the corner from success. You never know where your corner is, so just keep going.

11. The Certainty of Uncertainty

Life is what happens while you are making other plans. You can have faith in uncertainty; it's inevitable, consistent, and dependable. Frustration, anger, impatience, or dismay will not deter or postpone the manifestation of uncertainty.

You're driving down the road and the car in front of you unexpectedly jams on its breaks. What do you do? If you don't want to get into an accident, you slow down. It's irrelevant that you didn't plan on the other driver hitting his breaks. Once he does, you have to change, adjust, and adapt.

You are at the airport waiting to board your flight and there's an announcement that it's been cancelled. No matter how angry you get, the airline will not reinstate the cancelled flight. Your only alternative is to modify your travel plans accordingly.

Nature also provides us with examples that illustrate how to handle unexpected challenges. Watch water flowing through a small stream. What happens if you toss in a rock? Without any hesitation or delay, the water changes course and flows around the stone.

Throw in another rock and the water again reacts the same way. Remove one of the stones and the water readjusts and flows through the space that was previously occupied. The water doesn't care how many times its path has to be modified to circumvent obstacles. It simply takes the necessary action.

Getting through each day involves adjusting to numerous unplanned events. Usually these are small occurrences that you don't really pay attention to. Dealing with major unplanned events is the same as dealing with the minor ones.

The strategy is to evaluate, adjust, adapt, and keep going. What other choice is there? To effectively cope with uncertainty, you must accept that its appearance is inevitable. By expecting the unexpected, you won't be surprised when it occurs.

Flexibility and adaptability are your allies in accommodating uncertainty. When faced with the unexpected or unpredicted, behave like water and flow around the unanticipated events. The unforeseen has already occurred, nothing can change it.

Immediately begin to identify the best course of action in response to unforeseen events. With practice you can condition yourself to remain unshaken by surprises. When someone is forced to suddenly deviate from their plans, they can become distraught, angry, resentful, impatient, impulsive, or hateful.

Success, to a large extent, is determined by the ability to grow when faced with the unexpected. For example, in business those organizations that promptly adjust to unpredictable and changing environments will survive and thrive. On the other hand, many companies that are lethargic and slow to adjust will fade into oblivion.

Some people seem to have "bad luck" due to the way they respond to challenges. Others appear to have an uncanny ability to handle anything without missing a beat. No one is singled out. You choose which category you fall into.

Every unpredictable event has within it a gift of opportunity. If you develop an attitude of "OK, so where do I go from here?" you will have taken the first, and most important, step to adapt to the unexpected.

Rather than being apprehensive about uncertainty, consider it an aspect of living that prevents you from getting bored. It is your mindset that determines whether something is a stepping stone or a stumbling block. Your reality is based on your perception.

The unpredictable will occur without fail. The more you resist it, the more stress you will experience. You may as well make the best of it.

12. Tough Times Don't Last

Tough times don't last but tough people do. Problems and people are in constant conflict. The way you triumph over problems is by outlasting them. Adversity comes and goes. Problems are solved, resolved, or fade away. Tough people keep going. They may slip, trip, or fall. But they get up, recover their balance, and keep moving forward.

Tough times can have a grinding, draining, and demoralizing effect on a person. Allowing a tough problem to beat you into despair puts you in danger of becoming overwhelmed with little hope of recovery. Everyone needs encouragement and motivation. The following poem has hung above my desk for years:

Don't Quit
When things go wrong as they sometimes will;
When the road you're trudging seems all uphill;
When the funds are low and the debts are high;
And you want to smile, but have to sigh;
When care is pressing you down a bit -
Rest if you must, but don't you quit.
Success is failure turned inside out;
The silver tint of the clouds of doubt;
And you can never tell how close you are;
It may be near when it seems afar.

So, stick to the fight when you're hardest hit -
It's when things go wrong that you mustn't quit.
- *Author Unknown*

Reading this poem recharges my energy and enthusiasm. Often, it's when you're hanging on by your fingernails, and feel you can't last much longer, that you're about to turn the corner and overcome your problems. It's exactly at the point where you want to give up and throw in the towel that you must dig deeper into your inner storehouse of resolve and march on.

Understanding that tough times don't last gives you the stamina to outlast them. There has never been a problem that could stand up to the power of imagination and determination. Mental toughness empowers you to find solutions. Tough times force you to develop your strengths and formulate a strategy of thinking enabling you to find the way around, over, under, or through a problem.

Problems are temporary aberrations on your path of life. Tough times are like a brick wall. When examined up close, both are made up of small pieces that are removable. If you try and break through a brick wall by repeatedly throwing your body against it, you will only become sore and frustrated.

However, if you climb to the top of the wall with a hammer and a chisel, you can readily begin removing one brick at a time. This approach allows you to tackle tough times. Each challenge is simply a collection of bricks that can be removed one by one.

You can cause problems to crumble by disassembling them into small pieces. Once your brick wall of problems has been reduced into a pile of rubble, it no longer seems imposing or overwhelming.

When viewed in this way, every challenge will appear conquerable. You realize that you can overcome any obstacle. As you begin to proactively disperse adversity, your self-confidence, self-esteem, and mental toughness will flourish. Rather than being apprehensive of tough times, you will become as worried about them as you would be of a housefly. They may be annoying but they are certainly no match for you and the power of your mind.

You have the ability to be constant and consistent. You have the force of willpower and determination. Tough times will come and go but you have the capability to endure and overcome. You are a tough person who will outlast tough times.

13. Lessons from Nature

There are many phenomena in nature that embody the same principles applied to live without limits. We can observe inspirational examples throughout the ecosystem. While our minds distinguish us from the rest of the animal kingdom, we can still be motivated by the incredible lessons from nature.

Determination

The migration of various species is nothing short of amazing. The vast distances they cover illustrate the awesome power of determination. Although the exact methods used for navigation aren't completely understood, without determination there would be no success.

Each winter, monarch butterflies migrate thousands of miles from the northeastern U.S. to Mexico. They fly at an average speed of 12 mph as they head for Mexico's Sierra Madre mountains. The arctic tern travels farther than any of the other migratory birds. Twice a year, the terns fly between the Arctic and Antarctic, a journey of about 12,000 miles each way.

You can harness the power of determination. Set your sights on a goal and resolve to attain it. Do what it takes. Obstacles become impediments only if you stop when they are encountered. The way to reach the top of a mountain is to climb up the side, there's no shortcut. If a butterfly can fly thousands of miles, what is it that you can't do?

Persistence

Events appearing to be inconsequential in the short term yield extraordinary results when given enough time. Consider raindrops falling on a rocky mountainside. Surely the stone, which took thousand of years to form, would be unaffected by rain.

Yet, the rock of the Grand Canyon was eroded into the magnificent formation we see today by the relentless action of water. Ancient mountain ranges have been leveled over time by rain. Virtually every topographic feature of the earth has been shaped by the persistent action of water and wind.

Many people give up on their dreams due to impatience. Anything worth while takes effort and persistence. The larger the task, the greater the effort and persistence required.

Flexibility

During a storm, what's the difference between blown over trees and those that remain standing? The surviving trees are often the ones that bend and move in response to the wind. After the storm, the ground is littered with broken trees that were rigid and brittle.

Flexibility is a key element of survival. Flexibility enables you to adapt and change strategy as conditions warrant. If you find your path at a dead end, you must be flexible enough to change direction and map a new route to your destination.

Planning

Without planning ahead, animals wouldn't survive. Squirrels start gathering and storing food well before the winter sets in. Animals that hibernate begin eating extra food to build up fat reserves while food is plentiful and prior to the arrival of cold, severe weather. Birds start constructing nests before they have to lay their eggs.

Through proper planning you prepare for future needs. The opposite of planning is crisis management, where you do whatever is necessary just to make it to tomorrow. Taking action before the need is critical is the foundation of planning.

Change

Everything in nature changes. The weather varies daily. Landscapes change over time. Rivers and streams alter their courses. Floods come and go. Everyday something is different. Nature thrives on change. Each change brings new opportunities. When a tree falls during a storm, it provides a new habitat for plants and animals. Leaves dropping in the autumn enrich the soil.

Change is constant. It's nothing to fear and there isn't anything you can do about it anyway. Change is a perpetual source of endless possibilities. Without change, growth would be impossible. Watch for the opportunities revealed by each change.

Nature is replete with examples of the qualities needed to live without limits. Observe, learn, and apply nature's principles to enrich your own life.

14. All We Have is Today

Yesterday is over, that's why it's called the past. Tomorrow is unknown, that's why it's called the future. Today is a gift, that's why it's called the present. Life occurs exclusively in the present. Every morning you wake up in the present. It's impossible to wake up in the past or the future.

The past is gone forever, never to be changed. Lamenting the past or worrying about the future is a waste of time and energy. What you do today is the only thing you can control.

Bemoaning what you should have, could have, or would have done is a common pitfall. Expending any effort on this robs you of time that you can be using today. How do you break free from the past? By analyzing and understanding it.

Do you find yourself continually asking, "why do these things always happen to me?" If you don't learn and grow from your past, you are destined to repeat it. An understanding of what has happened enables you to avoid repeating mistakes while duplicating successes.

From the past you can identify what worked and what didn't. Repeating behavior that gave you undesirable results is ludicrous. Obtaining different results than you had in the past requires you to take different action today.

You need to identify cause and effect relationships. An understanding of what happened and why is essential. If something happened that you didn't like, did your behavior cause it? If so, what can you do differently to produce a better outcome next time? If events occurred that were totally out of your control, what can you learn from the experience?

You are a full time student of Life University. Your past is your transcript. Each of your experiences is a seminar. Some seminars show you what works and others show you what doesn't. You never fail. Failure is only a seminar in what didn't work the way you planned.

Every seminar is filled with invaluable information. Unfortunately, not everyone takes full advantage of the benefits these seminars have to offer. When you fail to profit from your seminars you risk living in the past and getting caught in a recurring cycle of mistakes.

Patterns of behavior become ingrained easily and require effort to alter. But if you don't change your actions, you will keep getting the same results. Over the next ten years you can live ten full, exciting, rewarding years or you can repeat the same year ten times.

What about tomorrow? Do you worry about tomorrow? Worry is like sitting in a rocking chair; it's a lot of activity that doesn't get you anywhere. People often fail to take action because they erroneously believe that circumstances will somehow get better with the passage of time. When someone expects conditions to change, without their proactive involvement, they are usually disappointed.

Situations have a tendency to go from bad to worse when no positive action is taken to improve them. If you want your life to change, take action to change it. Today is when you must take the first step. The size of the step is irrelevant but starting now is imperative.

Time goes by too fast. Each year seems to accelerate faster than the one before. Although time can't be slowed down, you can live each day to its fullest. Today becomes tomorrow's yesterday. Take positive action today so that tomorrow you won't lament what you didn't do yesterday.

Despite your past, the future is yours to make into whatever you want. Regardless of your age, you will never be as young as you are today. Don't allow your past to pollute your present. Each new day offers a new beginning. Seize today and the future is yours.

15. Looking Forward with Hindsight

Emotional passion tends to decline with time. What seems traumatic today is often completely forgotten weeks or months later. Comprehending this concept enables you to spare yourself a lot of heartache. See if you can relate to any of the following scenarios.

Six months ago you had trouble finding your keys and were late for work. At the time, you felt agitated and upset. Chances are, you don't even remember the incident. Last year, at a business lunch, you spilled salad dressing on your shirt. You were so embarrassed when it happened but now you can just laugh at the whole episode.

Three years ago, you were on your way to the airport to leave for vacation. You got caught in a traffic jam and missed your plane. You were worried sick that your whole vacation would be ruined. However, when you finally arrived at the airport, the airline was able to get you and your family on a later flight. Your trip was wonderful and the traffic jam is a distant memory.

How often have you looked back on what seemed like misfortune at the time, and wondered how you could have been so aggravated? Has anyone ever said to you,

"Remember when you were so upset about..." and you couldn't recall the incident they were referring to? Did you ever have a fight with someone and later couldn't remember what the conflict was about?

Undesirable or unpleasant circumstances and events are a part of living. Something breaks, you loose something, you're late, you embarrass yourself, you forget to do something, someone laughs at you, someone doesn't like you, you get into an argument, or your car breaks down. The list of distressing situations is virtually limitless.

Some circumstances you have control over, others you don't. Many people constantly get tripped up by the small annoying aspects of life. Far more emotional energy is expended than is warranted. As a result, the enthusiasm for good and positive things diminishes.

Feelings fade as you put distance between yourself and commonplace events. If they don't disappear altogether, their intensity diminishes. The cliché that hindsight is 20/20 is recalled on a regular basis. So why not look forward with hindsight?

What exactly does this mean? You have already experienced the effect time has on your memory. In hindsight, you may wonder why you were ever so upset. View the present as if you were looking back on it from the future.

When faced with a stressful situation ask yourself, "How will I feel about this next week, next month, or next year?" Although your feelings may be very intense at the moment, will they last? Recall how time has soothed past events. Consider the big picture. In the overall scheme of things, will what you are confronting now matter as much in the future?

When faced with feelings of frustration, project yourself into the future. In the future, what you are currently facing is at best a faded memory. Next, reassess the significance of what you are now experiencing and put it into perspective.

Since memories and feelings are going to fade anyway, why not save yourself a lot of time and grief by not getting trapped initially? The essential question to ask is "Will this matter to me later?" If the answer is no, why should you let it matter to you now?

That's how to look forward with hindsight. You view the events of today as if they were already in the past. Emotions diminish and fade with the passage of time and life goes on. Don't waste time now on those things that won't matter to you later. Spend time on what does matter.

BRYAN GOLDEN

16. Education Never Ends

If you think education is expensive, try ignorance. Knowledge is power. A common misconception is that education ends with graduation. Just the opposite is true; graduation is when education begins, that's why it's called commencement.

One of the most important things that school teaches is that you can learn. To learn is to grow. You should strive to learn every day of your life. Education is truly a lifelong endeavor.

Not all knowledge is equal. Knowledge is either useful or useless. Accurate information can be invaluable. The application of inaccurate or wrong information is detrimental and harmful. Knowledge is useful if it helps you achieve your goals and get the most out of life. You must be vigilant not to fill your mental space with lots of information that doesn't help you.

Useful knowledge can be broken down into several categories; knowledge needed to be successful in your occupation, knowledge needed to function in society, and knowledge needed to achieve your goals.

Knowledge needed for your job can be found in various places. You can take classes, read books, listen to tapes, watch videos, take on-line courses, or apprentice. All approaches to learning are effective so long as your information is accurate and current. Everyone has their own preferences as to which method works best for them. Find and utilize the methods that work for you.

Seek to become an expert at whatever you do. Experts always command the best pay and get to write their own ticket. Learn as much as you can about your occupation, even if you don't get paid for it. When you learn, you are investing in yourself. Study the leaders in your field. If you spend just one hour a week enhancing your knowledge you will rapidly improve your proficiency.

Jim, a shop owner, was watching one of his competitor's employees. He had observed the saleswoman's extraordinary level of professionalism, courtesy, and enthusiasm. Jim remarked to a friend that the woman would soon be getting a raise. When the friend asked Jim how he knew, Jim replied "If her current employer doesn't give her a raise, I will."

Regardless of your current occupation, possessing excellent written and verbal communication skills is essential. This requires a solid vocabulary and a good understanding of grammar. Anytime you interact with others you will be judged by what you say and write. Without these skills you severely handicap yourself by limiting your ability to effectively communicate.

Being able to communicate effectively will open many doors and you won't feel frustrated that people don't understand you. If your communication skills are lacking, start improving them immediately.

Functioning well in society is often a challenge since there are so many personalities to deal with. You can't control other people's behavior; you can only control your own. There are some simple, effective approaches that can be utilized regularly.

Treat everyone with respect and dignity. Don't be condescending or humiliate others. Everyone is equal. No one is below or above you. Never be rude or impolite. Projecting a sincere regard for others will elicit reciprocal behavior.

Don't get drawn into someone else's problems or allow others to push your buttons. Allowing yourself to be manipulated by someone else's behavior diminishes your ability to act thoughtfully and intelligently.

One of the best ways to learn is by helping others solve problems. By devising solutions for someone else, you refine your own problem solving abilities. A useful technique is to assist someone who has the same problem as you. It's not unusual to be able to devise an innovative solution for someone else even though you are struggling to solve your own problem.

Everyone has something to teach you. Always keep an open mind because the pool of knowledge is bottomless. Once you close your mind you cease to learn. Be a sponge for new information. You learn by listening, not talking. Watch, listen, read, learn, and grow.

17. Ask Questions

At a family reunion one summer, Alice, an eight-year-old, watched while her mother Fran prepared a roast for the oven. Alice observed Fran trim about two inches from each end. After Fran had put the roast in the oven Alice asked, "Mom, why did you cut the ends off?"

Fran thought for a moment then replied, "That's what my mother always did and so that's how I do it now." "But what's wrong with the meat at the ends?" Alice retorted. "I don't know. I never really gave it much thought. Let's ask your grandmother," Fran responded.

Alice and Fran went outside to find Grandma. "Grandma, why did you always cut the ends of the roast off?" blurted Alice. Grandma laughed and answered, "That's because the old oven that I had was too small to fit the whole roast."

Do you understand why you do the things you do? Do you take a particular approach to life because that's what you've always done? Do you comprehend the reasons for your actions? Do you continuously search for ways to improve your life? Everything is open to change and improvement.

Dr. Jonas Salk, who developed the polio vaccine, spent his childhood asking questions. By the late 1940's, polio was killing or disabling more than 40,000 Americans a year. Other researchers hadn't been able to develop a vaccine.

Dr. Salk, at a meeting of scientists, questioned the research methods being used. He was reprimanded, "You should know better than to ask a question like that!" Had Dr. Salk not asked the questions he did, he probably wouldn't have developed the polio vaccine and saved so many lives.

Rod Serling created "The Twilight Zone" television series in 1959. He had been asking why there were no TV shows on important, serious topics such as bigotry, the cold war, and alienation. His colleagues thought he was crazy when he left a $250,000 movie-studio deal to develop his TV show, which addressed those themes.

The founder of Avon, David Hall McConnell, observed that because women at the time (late 1800's) worked primarily in the home, they couldn't get to the stores often to buy beauty supplies. McConnell asked, "Why not bring the store to them?"

Continually asking questions enables you to determine whether you are on the right course or if corrections are needed. Questions allow you to determine why, when, where, and how. Without this information it's difficult to have a direction, purpose, and focus.

Life is cause and effect, action and reaction. Questions enable you to identify the causes. For different results you must take different actions. There are no shortcuts. You don't want to blindly stumble through life feeling as if you have no control. Questioning forces you to open your eyes and develop an awareness of why you are where you are.

When it involves you, ask others why things are done a certain way. Some people may get offended if you question why. If they do, it's their problem, not yours. Those who are secure and confident in what they do don't get offended or develop an attitude when questioned.

Learning, growth, and innovation occur because questions are asked and answers are sought. Developing a strong sense of curiosity will motivate you to constantly ask questions. The more questions you ask, the more you learn.

18. Information Overload: Avoiding Burnout

Cable TV, satellite TV, hundreds of channels, the internet, millions of web sites, radio, books, and magazines. You are flooded with information on a daily basis: news, advice, opinions, and knowledge. Who's doing what, what's happening to who, reality shows, fantasy shows. Information exists on virtually every topic.

Information overload can easily overwhelm you. The internet is a particularly insidious trap. When you're on-line, hours can slip by before you know it, without any measurable benefits. There's a staggering amount of information that, although fascinating, interesting, and intriguing, is useless.

How do you avoid overload and burn out? Apply a triage approach to sorting through information. Information can be divided into three categories. The first category is for information that is essential or helpful to your life. The second category is for information that is of no practical value whatsoever. The third category is information that can cause you harm.

Essential information enables you to move closer to your goals, to help others, to be more productive, to make your life better, or to make the lives of others better. This is the type of information you want to actively seek out.

Information of no practical value is anything that, although interesting, you wouldn't suffer without. The majority of information falls into this entertaining but useless category. Although there's nothing wrong with this type of information, time spent on it is time taken away from pursuing your goals.

The third category, information that causes harm, depression, or stress, is the most dangerous. Unfortunately, much of the daily news falls into this category. Typically, bad news gets much more coverage than good news. Immersion in the daily flood of bad news can sap you of motivation and drive. A quick skimming of headlines will keep you informed without becoming as drained.

Inaccurate or wrong information also falls into this third category. Relying on bad information to guide you toward your goals will have disastrous effects. It's like following a roadmap that shows a highway where in reality there is a cliff.

Use discretion when seeking out information. To assess the accuracy, reliability, and validity of any information, you must know what the source is as well as its credibility. It's difficult to find the jewels of objectivity and truth in the sea of information. The time required to sift through the garbage is well worth it.

Your time is finite. The amount of memory you have for absorbing new information is also finite. So you must be discriminating when deciding what information to expose yourself to. Information can be intoxicating. You can sit and subject yourself to it without having to expend much effort.

Information overload can stimulate a multitude of emotions. Depression, anxiety, frustration, and stress are a result of constant overexposure. At the very least, uncontrolled exposure to information robs you of time that could be better spent..

Goals are a valuable tool in deciding how to best utilize your time. When determining what information is truly useful, apply the goal test. If the information helps you move toward your goals, it is valuable to you. Time is so limited and whizzes by. Without constant vigilance, you'll expend it without realizing any meaningful benefit.

Be discriminating when deciding what information to focus on. Select that which helps you and makes you feel good. It's OK to tune out all the rest.

19. A Healthy Mind

Keeping your mind in shape is as essential for good health as exercising your body. Like muscles, your brain will atrophy and become soft without constant use. For peak mental performance your brain requires continual challenge and exercise. The more you use it, the sharper it will be.

Activities involving learning, problem solving, imagination, and visualization stimulate your mind. You will derive benefits that substantially exceed the effort expended. Your health, attitude, vitality, and overall quality of life will be enhanced. The brain, your control center, exerts a powerful influence over every aspect of your existence.

Among many other things, aging is strongly influenced by your state of mind. An active, alert, and sharp mind keeps you feeling young and vital. There are many examples linking all aspects of physical health to your mental state.

Education is a growth stimulant for your brain. Those who continually learn, maintain a greater a level of mental acuity compared to people who don't. There are now more opportunities and forums for education than at any other time in history. You can read, take courses, utilize the internet, watch educational videos, or listen to cassettes or CD's.

Thousands of courses, on virtually every subject, are available on-line without ever having to visit a classroom. Exposure to a number of diverse, unrelated topics will keep your mind challenged.

Expanding your vocabulary is an excellent way to give your brain a workout. There is ample evidence to suggest improving your vocabulary can actually increase the effectiveness of your thinking. People judge you by the words you employ when communicating.

There are many ways to easily enhance your vocabulary. Read copiously, looking up any words that you don't know. Utilize a vocabulary book or listen to vocabulary building tapes. Your word processor's thesaurus is an excellent tool to discover a wealth of synonyms.

Challenge your mind by actively engaging in problem solving. Everyone has problems. But many people endeavor to avoid or ignore their problems rather than solve them. Practice brainstorming. Phrase a problem as a question and write it down at the top of a sheet of paper.

For example, your problem may be that you don't have enough time to accomplish everything you want to do each day. You could express the problem as, "How can I free up more time each day?"

Be as clear and specific as possible. Write down as many answers to your question as you can think of. Formulate solutions as if anything is possible. Don't limit yourself by omitting an answer because you feel it's not workable or practical.

When you feel you've come up with every possible solution, try to think of at least one more. More often than not, this process will enable you to solve many problems whose resolution might have otherwise seemed elusive.

Preprogram your mind's subconscious to solve your problems. Take advantage of your mind's 24 hours a day activity. Just before going to sleep, think about your problem and possible solutions.

While you are sleeping, your subconscious mind will be working on solving the problem. Often, solutions will present themselves when you least expect it. Usually these solutions will emerge while you are not thinking about your problem at all.

Get in the habit of challenging and using your mind and you will reap perpetual benefits. There is much truth to the adage that age is a state of mind.

20. Control Your Own Emotions

Only you have complete control over your thoughts and emotions. However, many people do not fully exercise this control and thus inadvertently allow others to affect the way they feel.

From examples set by family and friends, to conduct shown on TV and in movies, society is replete with instances of individuals being manipulated by the actions of others. As a result, you learn to handle conflict by reacting with your emotions rather than your mind.

How many times have you heard any of the following? "He makes me so mad." "My husband would make me so happy if he would just listen." "My boss makes me upset when she treats me like that." "My kids make me so angry when they don't behave."

These statements are made because people believe others control their emotions. The longer this belief is held, the more someone will be influenced by what others say, think, or do.

You can't control other people and there are many circumstances that you have no influence over. While you can't control your environment, you can control your reaction to it.

Imagine you are walking down a trail in the woods and trip over a log. If you get angry at the log will it move out of your way? Does the log care how you feel? Your anger is a poison to you.

Anger will cause you to become tense and engage conflict. If you don't want to trip over the log again, you must watch out for it and step over or around it the next time it's encountered.

People and circumstances in your life are logs across your path. Each person does things differently than you might. You won't change their behavior but you can manage your reaction to it.

As another example, how would you respond to someone cutting you off in traffic? Would you get emotional, lay on your horn, possibly try to cut them off in return to teach them a lesson? Instead, relax and recognize that the other driver has a problem. Don't let someone else's problems or behavior become yours. No one can affect your emotions unless you let them.

How do you keep from being influenced by the actions of others? Start by not reacting with your emotions and not responding in kind. If someone yells at you, don't yell back, lower your voice. If someone threatens you, don't threaten back. Very often you can maintain control of a confrontation without responding at all.

Consider whether someone else's behavior requires any action from you. If not, then just remove yourself from the situation. When verbal input is required, present it in a calm and quiet voice.

If a response is warranted, you are not racing the clock to provide it. Before responding, pause, breath, and think before saying or doing anything. By reacting too quickly, you run the risk of not engaging in the most productive or beneficial behavior.

As soon as you find yourself in a situation where no matter what you say, the other person doesn't "get it," stop trying to make them get it and remove yourself. Although this is not necessarily the easiest thing to do, the alternative is to suffer and stress. Don't permit other people's problems to control you.

When you react with your emotions, the other person will engage you and continue to battle. Be like water, the harder it's grabbed, the more elusive it becomes. Learning to control your emotions takes constant practice but results in living with less stress and anxiety.

21. Guard Your Time

Time is a great equalizer. Everyone has the same amount each day. Time does not play favorites; it treats everyone the same. However, there is a wide disparity in how people use their time. Many people waste it as if life were a practice run. Time passes and is gone forever. If you don't use it wisely, there is no do over.

Do you feel as if there is not enough time to do the things you really want to do? Are there goals you could accomplish if you just had more time? Do you make the best use of the discretionary time you have?

Each day is loaded with potential distractions just waiting to drain your time. Time, which is one of your most precious assets, must be faithfully guarded. Would you permit others to walk through your home taking anything they wanted? Absolutely not. But do you allow other people and activities to rob you of your time? If so you are squandering something more priceless than any of your possessions.

Have you ever had time to "kill" while you waited for someone or something? If you start viewing time as the irreplaceable jewel it is, your outlook on how to spend it changes completely.

Rather than considering "down time" as an annoyance, view it as a gift of extra discretionary time. Use it for activities you find hard to fit in to your schedule. Carry a book, magazine, or newspaper with you and utilize any "extra time" for reading. You can use a cell phone to make or return calls. Use your imagination and you will discover various ways to utilize any "found" time.

You want to make the most of your time and use it for worthwhile activities. One way to determine what's worthwhile is to assess the affect it has on you. As a start, try applying the following tests to your discretionary activities.

Does what you do leave you feeling happy, positive, refreshed and energetic? Do you make progress toward you goals? Do you help someone? Do you learn or share? Are you or another person better off because of how you used your time? If one or more of these criteria are true, you have not wasted your time.

If you decide an activity isn't really worthwhile, don't waste your time on it. For example, what do you do during lunch? Do you eat with friends or coworkers who constantly complain about their problems? If so, do you go back to work after lunch feeling good and upbeat or do you feel drained and exhausted?

Rather than participating in a gripe session, try to get your lunch mates to focus on solutions instead of their problems. There's nothing stopping you from doing something different altogether. Why not spend your lunch reading positive, educational, or motivational material?

Do you commute to work? If you spend 30 minutes each way, you are spending 250 hours or 6.25 workweeks traveling. This time could be utilized listening to educational tapes or CDs. A 3-credit college course entails spending 45 hours in class. So each year you spend the same amount of time commuting as if you were taking 5 college courses.

How much time do you consume watching TV? If you average only 2 hours a day, you are spending 728 hours or 16 college courses in front of the tube each year. What about time you are now spending with social and volunteer activities? If there are other things you would rather do, you must learn to say no when invited or asked.

You don't have to overhaul the way you spend your time in one step. Start by trying to better utilize one hour a day and then go from there. Before you know it, you will be reaching many more goals and accomplishing more than you ever thought possible.

22. Patience

Patience: the capacity to endure hardship, difficulty, or inconvenience without complaint. Patience emphasizes calmness, self-control, and the willingness or ability to tolerate delay.
- The American Heritage Dictionary

You're driving home from work with 40 miles of highway ahead of you. Wanting to get home as soon as possible, you weave in and out of traffic doing 70 or maybe 75 mph rather than the 65 mph the rest of the traffic is traveling. How much time will you save? Zipping along at 75 mph saves you a whopping 5 minutes compared to 65 mph.

What are the costs? It takes much more focus and produces more stress and tension to weave in and out of traffic. And should some unsuspecting motorist happen to block your path, your frustration level rockets. Safety considerations or the risk of getting a ticket are some additional "benefits".

Once you get home, what do you do with your extra 5 minutes? You might sit down in front of the TV and do nothing to unwind. Perhaps you're so tense and irritable that you snap at your spouse and kids. Is it worth it?

74

At the grocery store, it's always your line that seems to move the slowest. Just as you're about to get to the cashier, the person in front of you has a pricing problem and the manager is summoned. You feel the stress and frustration building inside you. At least an extra 8 minutes crawl by before you finally check out.

Now you are in a bad mood and ready to tear into anyone that gets in your way. Why? Because you're really annoyed having had to wait an extra eight minutes and your patience is worn thin.

Each day, a variety of unplanned minor annoyances pop up. Such is life. There's no way to eliminate them. But there is a sure-fire method for attracting them: have no patience, a short fuse, and no tolerance. Alternatively, you can learn to adjust your reaction to these irritations so that they aren't so draining.

Flexibility and patience are inseparable. Try breaking a blade of grass by hitting it with a stick. The grass moves out of the way without any damage. Now strike a pane of glass. The glass shatters. A person with a low breaking point is like the glass.

How can you develop patience? When annoyances occur, react with "Oh well, no big deal." Look at unplanned or unexpected delays as an opportunity to develop yourself. It's found time, not lost time.

Be creative in utilizing this found time. You can use the extra time for thinking, an activity you can do anywhere. Think about solutions to problems or challenges you are facing. Think about your goals and formulate strategies to achieve them. Think about ways to improve yourself.

Carry reading material to use when you are delayed in waiting rooms, train stations, airports, or anywhere else.

Spend a lot of time in your car and it's inevitable you will be caught in traffic. Use your driving time to listen to books on tape or CDs. You can select fiction or non-fiction, on virtually any topic or genre. In this manner, your driving time is transformed into a personal enrichment session. Now when you get stuck in your car it becomes an opportunity for growth.

Spend unexpected "down time" doing something you feel is worthwhile and you'll eliminate the temptation to become impatient and frustrated.

23. Activity vs. Productivity

You're always busy. There's just not enough time in each day for all the things you need or want to do. You try to be as efficient as possible. It's as if you're on a treadmill. And no matter how fast you run, the treadmill is moving a little faster than you are.

You're exhausted at the end of each day. In spite of your hectic schedule, you are not really accomplishing what's important to you. You have goals but they are elusive.

You may feel frustrated. As you get busier, your irritation threshold drops and you react to minor irritations that never used to bother you. You're trapped in a vicious cycle.

There is a significant difference between activity and productivity. Activity is simply being busy. Activity doesn't necessarily correspond to accomplishment. You are productive when you are moving towards your goals. Activity is often mistaken for productivity.

Activity is safer than productivity. Since productivity involves working towards your goals, there is a perceived risk of failure. If pursuing one's goals is postponed, the chance of failure is also deferred. Being busy provides a sense of satisfaction.

Activity involves no risk. Nothing is on the line when you are engaged with chores, home improvement projects, errands, etc. Granted, some activities are a necessity. But there are many that are performed at the expense of pursuing your goals and dreams.

Many people don't feel any urgency to start pushing toward goals today. Starting tomorrow appears to be just as satisfactory. As this procrastination develops into a behavioral habit, goals are put off so often they begin to fade and may never be pursued at all.

Starting to work towards your objectives is just the beginning. To reach them, you have to pursue them consistently, on a regular basis, without being distracted or sidetracked. Pursuing goals in fits and spurts yields no measurable progress.

You engage in some activities for their recreational, enjoyment, or therapeutic value. These types of activities are good, worthwhile, and serve a valid purpose. However, when spending time on them, you are not working towards your goals.

It all boils down to what's most important to you. Without having any goals or dreams, how you spend your time isn't critical. But if there are aspirations you want to fulfill, it's imperative to be discriminating in how your time is spent.

Distinguishing activity from productivity requires you to identify your goals as well as the steps necessary to reach them. Once this is done, you have a way to decide how to best spend your time. Then you can monitor your time to assess if you are moving towards your goals.

Involvement in activities that serve as a distraction is known as displacement behavior. Anytime you choose behavior because it is a path of least resistance, you are engaging in displacement activity. Displacement behavior consumes a lot of time but doesn't move you in any particular direction.

As you become more selective in how you spend your time, you will start making consistent progress. Additionally, your frustration level will drop as you break out of the time trap.

Condition yourself to be productive and you will get more out of each day while elevating your mood and attitude.

24. The 80/20 Principle

Are all of your undertakings equal in terms of the results produced? Is there a way to leverage your time and effort to produce results four times greater than the energy expended? The 80/20 principle postulates that 20% of your efforts yield 80% of the results. Some applications of this principle are:

- 20% of the problems cause 80% of your frustration
- 20% of the people do 80% of the work
- 20% of the people cause 80% of your interruptions
- 20% of your friends and relatives will provide you with 80% of your support
- 20% of your recreational activities will provide you with 80% of your enjoyment

Although the percentages may not always be exactly 80% and 20%, the relationship between cause and effect is rarely balanced. Significantly more than half the results in life are produced from considerably less than half the actions. The aim is to utilize this principle to focus your energy on the 20% of the actions that produce 80% of the results.

What are the origins of this principle? In the late 1800's, Vilfredo Pareto, an Italian economist, found that 20% of the population owned 80% of the land. He observed that the 80/20 principle governed other relationships as well. For example, as an avid gardener, Pareto observed that 20% of the peapods in his garden yielded 80% of the crop.

Application of this principle can lead to dramatically increased productivity and much more efficient use of your time. You can make true progress by concentrating your energy on the 20% of the causes that produce 80% of the effects.

Addressing this 20% is not necessarily the easiest path. Many people apply the reverse of the principle. They spend 80% of their time and energy on those actions generating only 20% of the results. When confronting problems, the most readily resolved ones are frequently those yielding a minimum of relief. Human nature compels them to concentrate on the easiest obstacles first. As a result, they feel frustrated when there isn't enough time for everything they want to do.

For maximum effectiveness, you want to address the issues yielding the most substantial results. By focusing on the 20% of the activities yielding 80% of the results, you are essentially leveraging your time by a factor of four. Conversely, if you focus on the 80% of the activities that yield 20% of the results, you must work four times as hard to achieve your results.

Taking action without thinking and planning is the consequence of acting emotionally. Acting emotionally will lead you to address the 80% that yields 20% first. On the other hand, thinking through and planing your efforts, gives you the opportunity to do a cost benefit analysis ensuring that you are emphasizing the 20% that yields 80%.

The people who readily accomplish so much in one day, while you are overwhelmed, are most likely applying the 80/20 principle on a consistent and daily basis. "Plan your work and work your plan," is a timeless maxim. However, for ultimate results, modify it to read, "Plan your work to focus on the 20% that yields 80% and then work your plan."

25. The Slight Edge

"I'm a great believer in luck, and I find the harder I work the more I have of it."
-*Thomas Jefferson*

The slight edge principle is that a little more effort will produce a lot more results. Doing just a little extra, or going a little further, will give you a slight edge. For example, being two minutes early, rather than two minutes late, makes a big difference in a job interview. Doing more than is expected puts you ahead of the rest of the pack. Anyone can develop a slight edge.

There is often very little separating first, second, and third place winners. Yet, there is a world of difference in the benefits. In a horse race, mere inches can separate the winner. In a foot race, the winner can be hundredths of a second ahead of second place. A candidate will win an election if he or she has only one more vote than the runner-up.

The slight edge is gained by action, not necessarily innate abilities. Ironically, gifted people are not the ones who usually achieve the slight edge. It's those who are willing to put in the extra effort that do. Going the extra mile is far more powerful and effective than talent.

Desire is not enough; you must work for what you want. For maximum impact do more than is required or expected. This entails effort and persistence, but there is no other way. Thomas Edison once said that genius is one percent inspiration and ninety nine percent perspiration.

Any company that provides its customers with more than their money's worth will always be popular. You are in effect an independent enterprise. If you are an employee, you sell your time and services to your employer. If you have a business, you sell products or services to the public. Whatever your situation, you have competition.

Acquiring a slight edge provides a competitive advantage. There are two types of competition. You compete against yourself, for example, when you are in school and striving for good grades. You compete against others when you apply for a job, want a promotion, or operate your own business.

Consider yourself as your primary competition. To stay ahead, you need to continually learn, grow, change, and improve. If you stop pursuing self-development, you will stagnate, your slight edge will vanish, and life will pass you by.

The headlines are filled with examples of people and businesses that after developing a slight edge, rested on their laurels. In short order they were displaced by those who kept going. The fable of the tortoise and the hare has relevance for every aspect of life. This children's story embodies the power of a slight edge.

It's impossible to function in society without encountering competition. Many try to get by doing as little as possible.

They cut corners at every opportunity. They do only what is expected, if that. Do just enough and you will be trampled by those willing to do extra.

Be different. Do what others don't. Be a little early. Stay a little late. Take initiative. Understand what needs to be done, and do it without being asked. Invest in yourself. Enhance your knowledge, skills, and expertise.

Provide more than you are being paid for and your compensation will grow. Service precedes rewards, not vice versa. Because of the benefits that will ensue, it is more effective to do what's necessary to gain a slight edge instead of doing just enough to get by.

A common complaint is "Why put in extra effort when it's not appreciated?" If you put in extra effort it will be appreciated. If not in your current situation, then in another to which it will invariably lead.

To acquire a slight edge, give more than is required and you will receive more than you expected.

26. Have an Attitude of Gratitude

Focus on and be thankful for the many good things in your life. Take nothing for granted, recognize and appreciate everything. Every morning recharge your gratitude. Be grateful for everything you have, not upset over what you feel is missing. What others do or have has no bearing on you.

Goals shouldn't diminish your appreciation for the moment. If all you do is concentrate on what you want, you sacrifice living and enjoying today. Future ambition is realized by taking successive steps in the present.

If you have enough to eat, a place to live, a way to get around, people who care about you, or people you care about, then you are wealthy. If you lack any of these elements, you must still be grateful for what you do have, while striving to obtain whatever is absent.

People tend to feel bitter or resentful for a variety of reasons. They believe something is missing from their life, things aren't going their way or they have been treated unfairly. These people frequently ask, "why do these things always happen to me?"

Life's problems tend to take hold of your mind and turn

your focus to what you think is wrong. You may start resenting those who appear to be better off. You're apt to dwell on things that you imagine would make your life better if you had them. If only you had more money, more time, a bigger house, a different car, a different job, a different boss, a different career, etc.

The news is filled with people who "have it all" and yet their life is a wreck due to depression, drugs, aberrant behavior, crime, or some other malady. These people have reached the pinnacle of their professions and are at a level that most people can only dream about. But if a person feels their life is lacking, it doesn't matter how much they have.

Once your attitude becomes one of deficiency instead of abundance and appreciation, you become controlled by feelings of frustration and feel like a victim. As this happens, a vicious cycle starts which becomes all consuming.

Being bitter or resentful makes things worse. People who are bitter frequently find that their situations deteriorate and their mental and physical health decays.

It's difficult, if not impossible, to achieve your goals while you are resentful. Regardless of what challenges might befall you, bitterness makes finding solutions much more elusive.

There is no benefit to feeling bitter since it accomplishes nothing, harms you, and makes things worse. One way to avoid bitterness is to fill yourself with gratitude on a daily basis.

Begin your practice of gratitude every morning as soon as

you wake. Every day that you wake is a great day. If you have any doubts, try missing one. Take inventory of everything, no matter how small or seemingly insignificant, that is good in your life.

If it helps, make a written list of all you have to be grateful for. Read this list every day. As you do this, you will build and reinforce your attitude of gratitude. Don't give any thought to what you think you don't have.

Keep things in perspective. Consider all the people who have overcome difficulties far worse than yours. Don't be consumed by your problems, there is always a solution. Maintaining an attitude of gratitude allows your mind to devise a resolution for your circumstances.

The first step to changing and breaking out of a negative cycle is to focus on all of the things you have to be thankful for.

27. What You Project You Receive

Do you know anyone who always seems to have bad luck? Nothing ever goes right for them. Conversely, have you observed people who always wind up OK despite what befalls them?

What differentiates these two types of people? Their attitude, thoughts, and actions are as different as day and night.

You are a magnet. Your attitude, thoughts, and actions determine what you attract. Like attracts like. If you are negative, rude, and inconsiderate, this is what you will attract. If you are positive, upbeat, courteous, caring, and considerate, you will attract the same.

The effects of your actions always come full circle. How you treat others will determine how you are treated. You never know how long it will take, but what you project is invariably returned to you.

When you're feeling bad, annoyed, or frustrated you mustn't treat others poorly in response. Doing so is like throwing a rubber ball at a brick wall; it will bounce right back at you. How does someone react if you are rude? Chances are they will be rude in return. If they are, the situation will most likely escalate.

What should you do if you are not treated properly? First of all, don't respond in kind. If you do, you allow yourself to be drawn into the other person's problem, which will have a negative impact on you.

If someone mistreats you, resist the temptation to get even. Their actions will come back to them; it's inevitable. If you try to retaliate, you get caught in a negative cycle and your actions will have a detrimental affect on you.

Think before you speak or act. Monitor and be aware of your attitude, feelings, and actions. Behave in the same way you want to be treated. This is particularly difficult when someone is treating you poorly. You will be amazed at how your "luck" changes when you change the way you act.

Smile regardless of how you are treated, what is happening, or how you feel. Smile, especially when you don't feel like it. It's hard to feel bad when you smile. Transforming a frown into a smile instantly changes what you project.

Treat everyone with respect and always thank those who help you. All people want to be appreciated. A sincere thank you invariably makes a person feel good. Don't tell people to do things, ask them. Even if you are in a position of authority, you will get a better response if you ask rather than tell.

Endeavor to help others whenever possible. When offering your assistance, don't do it with the expectation of getting something in return. Only through unconditional generosity will you put good things in motion that will ultimately be returned to you.

A change in attitude and approach always precedes a change in situation. If you think that you will feel and act better when things improve, you will be waiting for a very long time. To be successful, act successful. To be happy, act happy. To be treated well, treat others well.

You can never know when, where, or how, but you will receive what you project. Everything comes full circle.

28. The Treasure Within You

Within you is a vast treasure awaiting rediscovery. You have more power, potential, and capability than you realize. A sculptor looking at a piece of marble sees a figure waiting to be revealed. The sculptor's job is to remove enough stone to expose the silhouette.

What abilities, talents, and desires do you posses that are waiting to be uncovered? Why is it that inner treasures are not always obvious? Let's follow a person's development from birth to adulthood.

When a baby is born, he or she has no concept of fear, failure, or danger. We'll call the baby Alice. Her imagination and dreams are limitless. Yet, she's completely vulnerable to her environment.

Alice is totally dependent on her parents for food, shelter, and protection. As Alice grows, her parents teach her the dangers of her surroundings. She learns what she can't or is not allowed to do. There is little, if any, emphasis on teaching her how to fully realize her potential.

Alice starts school and begins her formal education. That process includes learning proper rules of behavior. Rules, by their nature, outline what is prohibited or unacceptable.

Again, little or no emphasis is placed on how one's potential may be fully realized.

Alice's education constantly imposes conditions. There are several interesting examples that illustrate the impact learned limitations can have. Put a flea into a small jar with a glass top. The flea quickly determines that there is a limit to how high it can jump. Remove the glass top and the flea, due to its conditioning, won't jump out of the jar even though it has the capability to do so.

Take a fish tank and divide it in half with a piece of glass. Put several fish on one side. The fish will hit the divider until they learn where the swimming limits are. Remove the divider and the fish will still remain on one side of the tank.

The educational system and societal constraints are the equivalent of the jar top and fish tank divider on Alice's development. Alice, like many other children, learn artificially imposed limits. Since she considers these limits real, chances are that Alice will never consider the possibility of going beyond them.

As Alice grows and interacts with others, she will be exposed to jealousy. People tend to be envious of what someone else accomplishes or what they have. Jealousy can manifest itself through ridicule, and alienation. If Alice shows ambition, unique abilities, or talents she may find herself being rejected by her peers. Since children crave acceptance, Alice will feel that there is something wrong with herself.

Each time Alice experiences a negative reaction, a layer of stone forms around her dreams. She finds it easier to go with the flow and be accepted rather than blaze her own trail. Alice finds it much easier to be a follower than a leader. She gets into the habit of suppressing any desires to innovate.

Alice finishes school and begins working. She may not be doing the kind of work she once dreamed of due to all of the limitations imposed on her while growing up. Even though she is unhappy at work, Alice, because of her "education," understands that she has to be realistic and accept her situation.

If Alice shows too much enthusiasm or ambition at work, she may be admonished by her coworkers. She could be denied a promotion while someone less capable moves ahead because they are more adept at office politics. It's not unusual for a manager to feel intimidated by a talented and enterprising employee. Once again Alice learns that she is penalized for her efforts to excel.

Alice might want to go back to school to further her education or change careers. Perhaps she wants to start her own business. Her family and friends discourage her from being "impractical." Once again, a layer of stone is added as she receives little or no encouragement. Alice's dreams, aspirations, and abilities become so deeply buried that she forgets they ever existed.

Everyone has a buried treasure waiting to be rediscovered. What is yours? Uncover your dreams, aspirations, and goals and your life will be enriched in unimaginable ways.

29. Inspirational Dissatisfaction

Below are some examples of what can happen when you become complacent and too comfortable. You take your situation for granted and are poorly prepared to adapt to a changing environment. Complacency is a trap. It's the enemy of growth and innovation. When caught, you stagnate, stop creating, discovering, and growing. Life has too much potential to allow yourself to become apathetic.

Example 1. You have a great job and a wonderful boss. Working for a large corporation that's been in business for years, you're confident your position is stable. You have seniority and know exactly what needs to be done to keep everyone happy. You're well liked by your co-workers, are always on time and reliable. You're very comfortable and secure with your situation.

You take your job for granted. Life is routine and dependable. Then the unexpected happens with one of the following possible scenarios occurring. Your great boss leaves the company and is replaced by someone you can't stand. The company is taken over and your position is eliminated. The business is hit by an economic downturn and you are laid off. Your department expands, hires new people and you don't enjoy working with them.

Example 2. You've been married for 10 years to a wonderful person. Feeling very happy and content with your relationship, you take your spouse for granted. Life has become comfortable and routine. You've stopped making the extra effort to please that you did in the beginning. One day, in the middle of a disagreement, your spouse starts complaining about how insensitive you are and how you don't show the same attention you used to. You are in shock. You thought everything was perfect.

Example 3. You own and operate a business. It took a lot of hard work starting from scratch and making it successful. Fortunately you don't have any competition. As a result, you have become somewhat lax over the years. You no longer seek new and better ways to serve your customers and are not as attentive to their needs as you had been. Now that your business is successful there's really no need to push. After all, you're the only game in town.

Then, seemingly out of the blue, a direct competitor opens up. The new business does everything necessary to be successful. The prices are as low as possible and the customer service outstanding. Your business starts declining. Not only is new customer traffic down, but long time customers are leaving you for your competitor. You don't understand what happened.

In the above examples, each person became lulled into a false sense of security. Developing a sense of inspirational dissatisfaction helps you to maximize your potential and stay alert to the multitude of opportunities available. Nothing is permanent. The more mentally prepared you are to adapt as needed, the more successful you will be.

Inspirational dissatisfaction means being grateful and thankful for what you have while striving to improve yourself, innovate, and create. Young children are the embodiment of inspirational dissatisfaction. With limitless reserves of curiosity, drive, and ambition, they continually ask questions, always wanting to know why and how.

To children, each day is a new challenge filled with limitless potential. They are never satisfied with the same daily routine and constantly require new challenges. They continually explore different ways of doing things.

There is always room for improvement. How can you be a better person? What can you do to help others? Examine the various areas of your life: family, friends, and work. Each day behave as if you are trying to make the best possible first impression.

At work, how can you make things easier, faster, and more efficient? With family and friends, what are you doing to demonstrate your appreciation of them? Life is ever fascinating and rewarding when you strive to keep your outlook fresh.

Develop a feeling of inspirational dissatisfaction and you will stay on your toes searching for ways to excel. You will be ready for change and thrive when it occurs.

30. Overcoming Fear

The effects of fear are far reaching. Fear can thwart success, obscure opportunities, inhibit personal growth, induce depression, and encourage inactivity. In the past, fear has served a vital function for the human species.

Fear of fire, pain, and death has been essential to mankind's survival throughout history. Fear was an important asset that helped an individual stay alive. We no longer live in primitive survival mode. Most, if not all, of the fears we experience hurt us instead of help. What are you afraid of? The following are some common fears:

- Fear of poverty
- Fear of failure
- Fear of rejection
- Fear of ridicule
- Fear of loss
- Fear of the opinion of others
- Fear of being different
- Fear of success
- Fear of the unknown
- Fear of loss of security
- Fear of old age

Overcoming your fears requires you go where you're

afraid to go and do what you're afraid to do. Others have already overcome whatever it is you're afraid of. If someone else can conquer the fear, so can you.

In order to live free, you can't allow fear to control you. To conquer fear, you need to understand its basis. Start by determining what you have control over versus what's beyond your control.

Don't expend any effort or energy on issues you have no influence over. Distressing over the price of gas, the economy, or the weather, etc. is pointless. Let's look at overcoming the fears you do have control over.

Fear of poverty can cause you to miss opportunities. For example, the prospect of changing jobs, changing careers, or going into business for yourself can be scary. To conquer any fear, consider the worst that can happen. Invariably, you will find that the worst case scenario isn't really that bad.

If you change jobs and it doesn't work out, you can change jobs again. If you change careers and you don't like the new career, you can go back to the old one or try another. If you go into business for yourself and it fails, you can always start a different venture.

As long as you don't throw in the towel, the chances of you falling into the depths of poverty are virtually non-existent.

Fear of failure can stop you from trying anything new. Sometimes events may not work out as intended. So what? Thomas Edison discovered 9,999 ways in which a light bulb wouldn't work before he found the one way it would.

People who succeed the very first time are the rare exception. Will you look back on your life and regret that you were paralyzed by fear of failure? Or will you be glad for all the things you did and the chances you took?

Fear of rejection can be debilitating. The desire for acceptance by others is ingrained from infancy. If you make decisions based on fear of rejection, you are doing what you think someone else would approve of, rather than what you want.

Whatever you do, you will never please everyone, nor should you try. Do what you want and don't worry what other people will say, think, or do.

Fear of ridicule can prevent you from learning and growing. "What if other people laugh at or criticize me?," is a question that can stop you dead in your tracks. So what if they do?

Throughout history, everyone who ever accomplished anything was made fun of at some point. If you are being ridiculed, you're probably on the right track.

Fear of the opinions of others can divert you from pursuing your own goals. Does anyone care about what you think? Do other people seek your approval before taking action? The answer to both of these questions is most likely no. So why should you care about other's opinions?

Fear of loss can be paralyzing. It stops you from doing anything different. You're afraid to risk what you think you already have. You shouldn't act irresponsibly, but keep in mind that everything, including life, is temporary.

Usually the fear of loss is magnified in your mind and not based on reality.

Fear of being different is rooted in the perception that you are required to conform. You're told don't rock the boat, do what everyone else does. You fear that if you are viewed as different, you'll be shunned or outcast. Fear of being different causes you to follow instead of lead.

No two people are the same; everyone is unique. Don't compare yourself to others. Follow your own path. Better yet, make a path where none exists.

Fear of success can prevent you from achieving your dreams. Success doesn't change people. If someone is mean and rude, they will continue to mistreat people when they are successful. If you are kind and considerate, you can help people as you succeed. Success is wonderful, however you define it.

Fear of the unknown is as irrational as a fear can get. Nothing is known. Taken to the extreme, fear of the unknown can prevent an individual from leaving their home. The only certainty is uncertainty. Uncertainty provides a continuous supply of new opportunity. So, look forward to uncertainty, rather than being afraid of it.

Fear of insecurity is linked to fear of the unknown. Security is reliable, comfortable, and dependable. But nothing in life is like that. Security is an illusion, especially if you depend on others such as an employer, spouse, children, etc.

The only security you have is that which you create. The only person you can absolutely depend on is yourself. Many a person has been afraid to leave a "secure" job to look for other opportunities, only to be laid off or downsized. Believe in and depend on yourself. Whatever challenges befall you, you have the ability to take the necessary corrective action.

Fear of old age is pointless. Time goes by and there is nothing you can do to slow it down. Your age is determined more by how you think than by how many trips you've made around the sun. You determine how much living you pack into each day.

Recognize, understand, and overcome your fears. By so doing, you will free yourself from the anchors that are limiting you and will accomplish more than you ever thought possible.

31. A Kite Flies Against the Wind

Given a steady wind and a properly balanced kite, the kite will soar to great heights. But if the nose of the kite is pointed downward, the same wind will send it crashing into the ground. Resistance to the wind enables the kite to gain altitude.

Just as wind can either lift a kite or destroy it, criticism can either motivate you to reach lofty goals or dissipate your drive. Those who criticize far outnumber those who achieve. Yet no statue was ever erected to a critic. Rather than seeking to appease and mollify critics, utilize their admonition to stay on track to reach your goals.

Criticism is human nature. Anyone can be a critic. Instead of creating or innovating, people find it easier to criticize. If you want to accomplish something, critics will line up with an endless number of reasons why you won't or shouldn't succeed.

Utilize criticism to reach great heights. Understand that when you are being criticized, you are in the company of all great doers. Throughout history, every great person has been a magnet for critics. When you follow the beat of your own drum, you rise above the sea of mediocrity. As you ascend, you become a larger target for criticism.

What kind of criticism do you think the following person would receive? He dropped out of grade school. He ran a country store. He went broke. It took him 15 years to pay off his bills. He married, but had an unhappy marriage.

He ran for congress and lost twice. He then campaigned for the senate but also lost twice. He delivered a short speech and the audience was indifferent. He was attacked daily by the press and despised by half the country.

How many would label this man a loser who would never make it? How many would judge this man as incapable of succeeding? Who was this man? Abraham Lincoln. What was the short speech? The Gettysburg Address.

Put yourself in this situation. After only three months of schooling your teacher informs your parents that you don't have the intellectual capacity to pursue an education. So you are taken out of school.

But you have an insatiable curiosity and want to make a living discovering and inventing. Would your dreams be disparaged? Might you be laughed at? Probably. However, Thomas Edison did reasonably well with only three months of schooling and an "inferior" mind.

Ponder the plight of this poor fellow. He had a radical new concept for transmitting information. His ideas were so preposterous that his friends and family tried to have him locked up in a psychiatric institution. Undeterred, in the 1890's, Guglielmo Marconi proceeded to successfully develop the radio.

Are you routinely chided or ridiculed for your dreams, desires, plans, or goals? If so, take a look at the background of the people who are offering negative opinions. Are they experts in the areas you are striving for? Have they already accomplished what you are trying to do? Are they presenting their "advice" because they want you to succeed? If the answers are no, why would you ever allow their criticisms to deter you?

How do you fly against criticism? Believe in yourself and your goals. You don't need approval. You aren't obligated to convince anyone that your ideas are worthwhile. Often it's prudent to keep your aspirations mostly to yourself. Seek out others who are also working towards their dreams and form a motivational group to help and support each other.

When you succeed, some people will tell you they knew you could do it. Others will insist you must have been lucky or were in the right place at the right time. These will be the very same people who were convinced you'd never make it.

Use criticism to feed your determination and strengthen your resolve. Make it the wind that will propel you to new and exciting achievements.

32. Your Choice

You don't need to feel depressed; you can choose happiness.

You don't need to be afraid; you can choose confidence.

You don't need to be discouraged; you can choose action.

You don't need to be stressed; you can choose tranquility.

You don't have to settle for failure; you can choose success.

You don't have to feel isolated; you can choose giving.

You don't have to be defeated; you can be victorious.

You don't have to follow; you can blaze your own path.

You have the gift of free will and control over your thoughts. Life is a journey comprised of choices. Each day is a new beginning full of unlimited potential. Let's examine each of the above choices and explore different strategies that enable you to make the most beneficial decisions.

Depression

There are many causes of depression and different levels of severity. Treatments can range from self-reassessment and behavioral modification to professional psychological or psychiatric therapy. One common theme is a feeling of unhappiness combined with gloomy thinking. Since your feelings are directly linked to your thoughts, begin by developing an awareness of what you think about.

When you find yourself engaging in unpleasant or negative thoughts, replace them with thoughts of joy and happiness. Recall events or people that made you happy. Visualize yourself in a favorite location where you felt relaxed and content. Imagine how you want to feel and envision yourself feeling that way.

Regardless of the cause or severity of depression, the more proactive you are, the more rapid will be your recovery.

Fear

Fear is concern over a particular outcome. It involves projecting the future through a "what if" scenario. What if I get hurt? What if it doesn't work? What will people think of me? What if something happens that I don't know how to handle? The most insidious aspect of fear is that it paralyzes and prevents you from taking action. Confidence is the antidote for fear. Confidence is enhanced by doing what you're afraid to do and going where you're afraid to go.

Rather than viewing fear as a limitation, consider it a challenge and a chance to grow beyond your limitations. Overcoming fear is worthwhile whenever there is something positive to be accomplished. Overcoming fear does not mean taking stupid risks that can be destructive to you or others.

Discouragement

A feeling of discouragement may result after repeated efforts with little results. Condemnation by others, a lack of support, or a perception that the odds are against you, will also lead to this feeling. Discouragement drains you of motivation and drive.

When faced with discouragement, many people give up. Yet, it is precisely at this point that it's essential to persevere and redouble your efforts. If you must adjust your strategy, then do so. But never, ever give up. Continue taking action and keep going.

Stress

Stress, anxiety, and tension seep in from the environment. Stress builds up gradually without your noticing. Before you realize it, you are wound up like a spring. Unless you take corrective action, you will become acclimated to increasingly elevated levels of stress. As this happens, you accept stress as normal and forget what true tranquility is.

Give yourself some private, uninterrupted quiet time each day. During this period don't try to accomplish anything. Spend the time with your eyes closed and mentally travel to a tranquil setting. Allow you body to relax while you take deep full breaths. Regularly engaging in this practice will be invigorating while reducing your stress.

Failure

There are many definitions of success. Yet, there is only one characterization of failure; giving up. Not everything you attempt will go as planned or as expected. Life is unpredictable and full of surprises. In an ideal world, you would be successful on the first attempt with whatever you try.

Everyone can be successful, but not everyone will. Why? Many people don't have the drive and endurance to stick with something until it works. Invariably, anyone who succeeds has weathered many unsuccessful attempts. Success requires persistence, patience, focus, determination, effort, and a refusal to quit.

Often people will declare something a failure because the desired results haven't materialized fast enough. There are countless stories of people quitting when they were just around the corner from success. If something didn't work it can be for one of several reasons: you didn't want it badly enough, you didn't give it enough time, or you needed to adjust your approach.

Since failure only occurs when you give up, if you don't want to fail -- don't stop trying.

Isolation

A feeling of isolation results from focusing on yourself and your needs to the exclusion of all else. Although it's imperative that you respect and care about your well being, you won't accomplish this by turning inward. People tend to disassociate themselves from and shun those who are perceived as selfish or conceited.

Genuine caring and concern for others is an antidote for feeling isolated. Once again, the rule that you get by giving applies. For example, on a social level, the way to be thought of as a good conversationalist is to be a good listener. People will take an interest in you after you take an interest in them.

Should you feel isolated, withdrawing and perhaps feeling bitter will only intensify your situation. Action always precedes results. Seek out situations where you can offer help and give to others, especially when you don't feel like it.

Defeat

Everything happens for a reason. With the proper attitude you will discover it. I'm a firm believer in this and have personally experienced it numerous times. Perception is often the difference between defeat and victory. Defeat is rich in educational value. Defeat can be transformed into victory by using it as a stepping stone to continue moving forward. Defeat is wasted when it causes you to give up.

Defeat is a seminar that can make you smarter and stronger. Every perceived defeat reveals new opportunities that were previously concealed. If you feel defeated, analyze what happened, why it happened, and whether or not you could have done anything different to change the outcome. Then determine where you should you go next and do so. Every defeat is another rung on your ladder to success. Keep climbing.

Following

Following may seem easier than leading, but doing so runs the risk of jeopardizing your own goals and desires. It may appear safer to follow than to take chances making your own decisions. However, a follower accepts the choices of others. A leader makes his or her own decisions.

By following you jeopardize your own analytical processes. You aren't fully exercising your abilities to appraise options and pick your own way. Your mind works best when it has to constantly evaluate and select the best course of action.

Each day you are free to make whatever choices you want. You are not trapped nor are you forced to make certain decisions. Recognize and take advantage of the tremendous influence you have over your life.

33. Impossible = _It_ _Means_ _Possible_

Erik Weihenmayer, 35 years old, has accomplished a lot. He's an acrobatic skydiver, a world-class athlete, marathon runner, long distance biker, scuba diver, skier and member of the college wrestling hall of fame. He's also climbed Mount Everest as well as the second and third highest peaks in the world.

These accomplishments would be considered exceptional for anyone. But Erik has been totally blind since the age of 13. How many people with sight would consider any one of Erik's accomplishments impossible?

Something is only impossible if you believe it is. All of the following were at one time considered impossible: electric lights, flying, radio, TV, space flight, SCUBA diving, computers, etc. Yet today we take these, and many other things, for granted.

Unfortunately, it's all too common for people to fail to attempt something under the guise that it's impossible. There are many justifications for declaring something impossible: "I don't have enough money," "I'm not smart enough," "I'm too old," "I'm too young," "I don't know the right people," "I don't have enough education," etc., etc., etc.

In 1830, he was born in a small town in N.Y. After finishing the eighth grade he set out on his own. At age 14, he made his way to Ohio where he landed a job as a store clerk earning $5 a month. Five years later, he was a store manager earning $400 a month. A short time later, he worked his way up to an executive position.

He went on to invest his entire net worth of $50,000 in a salt business. Within two years, the business failed. He lost his entire investment as well as another $50,000. Undaunted, he started again, from scratch, and did so well he was able to pay off all his debts within several years.

Later, investing in the fledgling oil industry, he applied the lessons he learned in the salt business and went on to become a co-founder of Standard oil. Then, in the 1880's, Henry Flagler started developing the transportation and infrastructure systems in Florida, a sparsely populated state considered by many to be worthless swampland.

In 1813, a 4-year-old French boy was completely blind as the result of an accident. At that time, blindness robbed an individual of the ability to work and destined him to the life of a beggar. Loss of sight precluded one from participating in the normal world of instruction and learning.

The boy's parents didn't want their son to be forever dependent on someone else. They didn't treat him differently because he couldn't see. The boy wasn't one to give up easily and learned to use a cane to navigate from one point to another.

He won a scholarship to the Royal Institute for Blind Youth in Paris when he turned 10. There, he worked to

BRYAN GOLDEN

develop a code system of raised dots and dashes that would enable blind people to read. By the time Louis Braille was 15, he had developed the reading system that is named after him and used today.

It's considerably easier and safer to declare a dream, desire, or goal as impossible rather than striving for success and falling short. Certainly, no one could be faulted for avoiding the impossible.

Each time you elude risk by evading the impossible, you lower the threshold for what you consider unattainable. Conversely, by accomplishing the "impossible", you raise the bar for what you can achieve.

By using the label of impossible to take the path of least resistance you are cheating yourself. The richness of your life is in direct proportion to the number of "impossible" tasks you are able to accomplish.

Instead of justifying why something is impossible, decide what you want to do, formulate one reason why you should do it, and go accomplish it.

114

34. Winning vs. Losing

Winning vs. losing. This concept is typically used to compare one person or group to another. There is one winner and the rest are losers. In the game of life, however, everyone can be a winner. The competition is not against someone else but rather you against yourself.

You are the contestant, opponent, coach, manager, trainer, owner, and referee. If you are striving to reach or exceed your potential, you are a winner. By striving to help others, being of service, and working to solve problems, you become a winner.

Look over the two categories below. Perform an honest self-assessment. Ideally, you want to have all of the attributes of a winner. If you don't currently possess all of the winner's characteristics, don't feel discouraged. There's nothing preventing you from steadily improving yourself and thus becoming more of a winner.

The Winner:
- Is always part of the answer
- Always has an action plan
- Says, "Let me do it for you."
- Sees an answer for every problem
- Says, "It may be difficult but it's possible."

The Loser:

- Is always part of the problem
- Always has an excuse
- Says, "That's not my job."
- Sees a problem for every answer
- Says, "It may be possible but it's difficult."

Everyone has unlimited potential. Growth and change only takes place through full understanding and recognition of yourself and you present situation. Enhancing your knowledge of yourself enables you to correct faults while enhancing and reinforcing strengths.

You have the ability and power to improve and modify your life at any time. If and when you do this, and how long it takes, is up to you. Nothing happens until you take the reins of your destiny.

Part of the answer vs. part of the problem -
Every problem or challenge has an answer or solution. Solutions are not always evident and are often elusive. But they are there. Look for the answer and you move forward. Complain about a problem, or take on the role of victim, and you regress. Refuse to believe there is a solution and you'll never find one.

Action plan vs. excuse -
A plan is your road map to personal development and overcoming challenges. An excuse is a path of least resistance that justifies why you are where you are. Formulating and implementing plans take more effort than concocting excuses but yield results far in excess of the energy expended. Excuses keep you a prisoner with no hope of escape. Action is your ticket to freedom.

Let me do it vs. it's not my job -
Take initiative. Don't wait to be asked or told. Seek to anticipate other's needs and provide assistance wherever and whenever possible. Taking initiative enhances self-esteem and builds you a reputation as someone who is reliable, dependable, and gets the job done. The demand for initiative takers always exceeds the supply.

An answer for every problem vs. a problem for every answer -
Every adversity carries the seed of an equal or greater opportunity. Innovators are the minority and critics are the majority. Yet no statue has ever been erected to a critic. Be an innovator and you will have little competition. Don't allow your thinking to be stifled by the negative opinions of others.

Difficult yet possible vs. possible yet difficult -
The degree of difficulty or energy required to solve a problem or accomplish something is irrelevant. Everything worthwhile takes effort. The greater the effort, the greater the rewards. You can achieve whatever you want in life by expending the necessary energy in an appropriate way.

Everyone can be a winner. Being a winner is not an accomplishment; it's a way of living. To remain a winner in life, just like in sports, takes constant training and practice. Challenges, problems, and adversity are the exercises that make winners stronger.

If you think like a winner and act like a winner, you are a winner!

35. Self-reliance

Self-reliance is taking action to shape the direction and quality of your life. Look in the mirror to meet the one and only person answerable for your well being. You are responsible for the position you are in.

Do you use one or more of the following to justify your situation: childhood, parents, siblings, spouse, friends, children, education, the economy, the government, skin color, height, weight, religion, where you live, your occupation, etc? If you do, you are deluding yourself into inaction by placing the blame for your circumstances on someone or something else. This line of reasoning absolves you of personal responsibility. If you're not the cause, how can you be accountable for the solution?

If you're not happy with your circumstances, you are the only one who can change them. No one else is at fault and no one else is responsible. Placing blame on external factors locks you into your current situation with no hope of escape.

You have a choice. You can make excuses justifying your current position or you can take charge of your life. There is no easy route. Anything worthwhile takes effort. Life is a challenge, but that's what makes it interesting. The following examples illustrate the awesome effectiveness of self-reliance.

Nellie H. Lee loved to write. She found that writing was the hardest thing in the world, yet it was the only thing that made her completely happy. In the 1950's she had to pinch pennies while she was working on her novel. She needed a desk and a typewriter. For a desk, she nailed wooden legs to a door. She found an old, broken typewriter and fixed it.

When Nellie sent her book to a publishing house in 1957, they returned it and told her to start over. For almost three years, she wrote, re-wrote and reworked her story. When Harper Lee's book was finally published in 1961, "To Kill a Mocking Bird" won the Pulitzer Prize.

In 1938, eight year old Ray C. Robinson had more justification than most to be bitter and curse his predicament. He lived in the Deep South, was black, blind, and soon to be orphaned. Yet young Ray wanted to be a musician. The easy route for Ray would have been to give up and no one could have blamed him. Everything was working against him: his disability, skin color, and where he lived.

Virtually insurmountable odds were no match for the young boy's determination and drive. Ray refused to be deterred by his limitations. Constant hard work and a relentless pursuit of his dreams paid off. The boy grew up to become one of the greatest rhythm and blues singers. Ray Charles earned 12 Grammy Awards and his recordings have sold tens of millions of copies.

One of Margaret Rudkin's children was diagnosed with asthma in 1935. A physician thought that a wholesome diet might improve her son's condition. Margaret decided to bake her own bread. She had never done this but was convinced she could accomplish anything she set her mind to.

Margaret persisted until she created a healthful and delicious bread. She started out baking only for her family. The doctor then asked her to make bread for him and his other patients. Margaret's bread quickly became popular and she started a modest business from her home.

Circumstances were not in Margaret's favor. She was almost 40, the nation was in the midst of the Depression, and she was intending to sell her bread for two and a half times the cost of a normal loaf. Additionally, in the 1930's, it was far from accepted for a woman to go into business. Margaret is yet another example of what can happen when a person takes responsibility for their life. Margaret named her business Pepperidge Farm.

Within you exists the desire, drive, and ability to seize control of your life and future. Don't waste another moment. Get in gear, get determined, and make progress, not excuses.

36. Nice People Finish First

Chances are that you've heard the expression, "nice guys finish last." Nothing could be further from the truth. This statement is used by many to justify less than ethical treatment of others. No one wants to finish last. Therefore, many act as if the end justifies the means.

Under the guise of not wanting to finish last, people engage in inconsiderate conduct. At best, this type of behavior will give the illusion of short-term gains. These apparent gains come with a high price; the forfeiture of building a solid foundation of living which will last a lifetime.

Being nice is not synonymous with subjugating your dignity or your right to be assertive. You don't have to allow yourself to be used as a doormat. Everyone, at one time or another, has been in a situation where they felt pressured to agree to do something they didn't want to do. You are not obligated to comply with the requests of others. It's OK to say no.

Being nice entails acting in a considerate, polite, respectful, and thoughtful manner. Being nice means not elevating yourself by stepping on others. Being nice requires understanding that you are not better than someone else and no one is better than you. Being nice compels you to help people without expecting anything in return. A true measure of character is how a person treats those who aren't in a position to do something in return.

Unfortunately, there are people who view being nice as a sign of weakness and an invitation to be taken advantage of. However, no one can take advantage of you without your permission and participation.

Your response when someone tries to take advantage of you sets a precedent that determines how you are subsequently treated. Unless you make your limits clear, people will continually try to push your boundaries. You can decline to go beyond your limits at any time without having to justify yourself or convince others.

Your boundaries will be tested on several fronts: at work, by family, and by friends. Each situation requires a different approach. At work you have an obligation to perform certain services in return for your pay. But when requests fall outside your normal job responsibilities, you must decide whether you want to or should comply.

It's not uncommon to experience direct or implied pressure insinuating your employment or advancement might be affected if you say no. This is a very uncomfortable position to be in, but it happens.

Be clear in your own mind what your limits are. You allow yourself to be held hostage if you are afraid to say no to unreasonable or inappropriate requests.

If you are so concerned by job security that you won't say no, you essentially broadcast that you have no limits. As a result, you will continually be taken advantage of. When appropriate, say no, and you will usually find that nothing bad happens and you are treated with more respect.

Requests from family and friends are somewhat different. Guilt and peer pressure is used to cajole you into doing what someone else wants. Exceed your boundaries and you will be taken advantage of repeatedly. Decline requests with politeness and a smile while being firm.

Be diplomatic by saying things like, "Thank you for asking, but I have a prior obligation" or "I've already made other plans" or "If you had only asked me sooner" or "Thanks for thinking of me but that's not something I'm interested in."

Sometimes you will decline a request because of the way you've been treated. If this is the case, don't express it as your reason for saying no. Take the high road and don't get caught in the trap of retribution. All that matters is that you don't do what you don't want to do. You are not obligated to justify your actions or explain yourself.

If you don't respect your own limits, no one else will. Demand respect and you'll receive it. Get in the habit of refusing to be taken advantage of.

37. Overcoming Adversity

Adversity is an unavoidable part of life. Death of a loved one, breakup of a relationship, malicious action by another, job loss, natural disaster, or any other undesirable event are all circumstances people encounter. Events happen that are beyond our control. As much as we would prefer to have lives free of adversity, it just won't happen.

Successfully overcoming adversity is essential for a healthy life. Conquering adversity builds mental strength, character, and endurance. You develop in ways that would not otherwise be possible.

When undesirable incidents occur, you want to avoid the pitfall of the past and becoming mired in the would of, could of, or should of trap. It's done and over. Adversity is overcome by moving forward.

Nothing you can do, say, think, or feel will ever change the past. Wallowing in feelings of guilt, regret, or despair diminishes the present and compromises the future. Although it's difficult to accept unpleasant events, you have no choice, they have already occurred. The goal is to adjust your outlook to enable you to regain your footing, function, and move ahead.

Adverse reactions are not unusual when faced with hardship. Feelings of denial, sickness, giving up, retribution, being overwhelmed, inactivity, anger, guilt, and "why me" are not uncommon. These reactions are counter-productive causing you to feel worse. Anger or bitterness poisons you and impedes your recovery. These emotions are usually automatic in response to distressful circumstances.

You have control over your reaction to adversity. You have been conditioned by how others respond to unpleasant circumstances. However, most people aren't a good role model for effectively dealing with adversity. You want to recondition yourself to respond in a manner that's helpful rather than destructive.

Adverse situations can be divided into three categories; events you have no control or influence over, situations resulting from decisions you have made, and circumstances caused by someone else's actions. Effort spent on lamenting the past drains you of energy needed to handle the present and plan for the future. Your energy is best spent ensuring that you will be OK.

After experiencing a loss, a period of grieving is normal but should not become a way of life. Everything in life is temporary. What varies is the timing. As much as you may miss someone, there are people who depend upon and need you. Focusing on the needs of others is an effective and positive way to move forward.

Perhaps you are unhappy with the results from your decisions. Everyone makes bad calls. There are no "do-overs" -- life goes on. How do you get back on track? Learn from your experiences and keep going. Inaction will cause you to feel worse.

Channeling your energy into positive action is one of the best cures for being disheartened. For example, if you've lost a job, immediately begin the process of getting another one. No matter how bad unemployment is, the odds are always weighted heavily in your favor. Even if the unemployment rate was an astronomical 15% you have an 85% chance of finding a job.

If a relationship has ended without any chance of reconciliation, take comfort in the fact that there are numerous people in the same boat. Get out, circulate, and meet people.

If you've made a bad decision and are unhappy with your circumstances, resolve to change direction. Effecting a correction can be difficult, but persisting in an unhappy state is torture.

Everyone encounters adversity. No one is ever singled out. No one knows why some things happen, they just do. Some decide to regain their footing, catch their breath, and keep walking forward. Others choose to give up.

Each time you overcome adversity you get stronger and wiser and can show others by example how to do it also.

38. Cause and Effect

Your reaction to the events around you determines how you feel and how you affect those you come into contact with. Consider the following example:

Jane, a bank executive, got caught in traffic on her way to an important presentation at a board of directors meeting. As a result, she was forty-five minutes late for her presentation. After the meeting Jane was in a really bad mood. Upon returning to her office she discovered that several expected reports were not there.

Jane called Kevin, her administrative assistant, into her office and reprimanded him for not ensuring the reports had arrived on time. Another department was preparing the reports. Kevin had no control over when they would be delivered. Jane was in a foul mood and she didn't want to hear any excuses.

Upset and stressed, Kevin called Donna, the secretary for the department preparing the reports. He started yelling at her that the reports that he had requested had not arrived. Although this was the first Donna had heard of the reports, Kevin didn't care. He was upset and took his anger out on Donna.

By the time she got off the phone with Kevin, Donna was seething. Who did Kevin think he was speaking to her like that? Just then, Ed from the mailroom called Donna to ask how she wanted a package shipped. Donna accused Ed of being an idiot for not knowing the package should be sent overnight because it was so important.

Ed tried to explain there was no way he could have known what she wanted. Donna just slammed the phone down in a huff. Ed was livid. Did Donna think he was a mind reader? Ed was still agitated as he went to the diner for lunch.

The diner was extremely busy. His waitress, Stacey, took longer than usual to take his order. Ed was annoyed with the slow service. He was rude to Stacey and left her a small tip. Stacy was running herself ragged and was offended by Ed's attitude and tip.

The rest of Stacey's shift seemed to drag. When she finally got off work, she was in no mood for any more hassles from anyone. As Stacey walked into her apartment, her five-year-old son, Jimmy, ran excitedly to greet her.

Stacey immediately noticed that Jimmy's pants were filthy. "I just washed those," she yelled. "Can't you keep anything clean?" Jimmy ran up to his room crying. His cat came over to him purring. Jimmy was so upset he kicked the cat.

Wouldn't it have saved a lot of people a lot of grief if Jane had gone directly to Stacey's house and kicked Jimmy's cat?

When you take out your frustrations on others you may be starting a cascading chain reaction. Once you initiate this series of events, you can't stop it. Nor can you know who or how many are indirectly impacted by your actions. Is this really the kind of influence you want to have on others? You don't have to be a conduit for negative energy.

If a person takes out their frustrations on you, break the chain by refusing to take it out on someone else. When you react negatively to another's behavior, you allow yourself to be drawn into their problems. You have control of your thoughts. If you feel annoyed, wait, think, calm down, and allow your emotions to settle before speaking or acting.

Words spoken or written, or actions taken are like arrows shot from a bow; once released they can not be recalled. Much less time and effort is required to think before acting compared to what is necessary to salvage damage inflicted by impulsive and emotional behavior.

Keep things in perspective. Let stress roll off you without grabbing hold of and internalizing it. Don't kick the cat.

39. Living Without Anger

The "benefits" of anger are many. Stress, anxiety, diminished judgement, reduced productivity, poor digestion, sleeplessness, elevated blood pressure, negative impact on relationships, unhappiness, and attraction of negative situations can all be yours just by being angry.

Anger repels people, destroys relationships, creates problems, intensifies problems, causes regret, burns bridges, and dissolves solutions.

Anger doesn't have to manifest itself via your behavior to be destructive. Anger that is internalized can be just as damaging. A fundamental misconception is that people, events, or circumstances make you angry.

Anger is a chosen reaction to your environment. As you allow anger to become a conditioned response, a downward spiral develops. Habitual anger feeds itself and increases in intensity over smaller and smaller matters. Without vigilance, resistance to anger diminishes and it becomes automatic behavior when faced with adversity.

Anger does not serve you. Regardless of your reasons for being angry, anger never resolves problems; it makes them worse. You can learn to manage and eliminate anger. Doing so requires a recognition, understanding, and acceptance of several concepts.

First, you and you alone are responsible for your emotions and behavior. No one has the power to make you angry. You create your own anger. Second, you must identify what arouses anger within you. Without recognizing what triggers your anger, there is no chance of you managing or eliminating it.

Some common causes of anger are: injustice, hurt, frustration, annoyances, being treated unfairly, being taken advantage of, a threat of loss, experiencing a loss, plans that don't materialize as expected, regret over the past, people don't behave as expected, or a situation that is out of your control. Each person has a different reaction to the same event. Something that makes you furious may not have any impact on others and vice versa.

Do you engage in behavior that evokes anger in others? You can become angry in response to someone else's anger and someone else may become angry in response to your anger. Anger is a vicious cycle that will rapidly escalate unless diffused by one or both parties involved.

There is no way to eliminate circumstances that make you angry. But you can manage your response in a way that prevents anger from taking hold. A thorough understanding of what makes you angry enables you to preplan alternative strategies for reacting.

If you are angry, don't make any decisions or take action until allowing the anger to subside. Acting while angry increases the probability that you will say or do something regrettable.

As soon as you find yourself becoming angry, identify the specific circumstances you are reacting to. Understanding the cause enables you to take steps to diffuse the anger and prevent it from escalating.

Having identified the source of your anger, determine what action can be taken to rectify the situation. You want to solve a problem, not be malicious. Revenge, punishment, mistreatment of others, or self-pity are not healthy motivations. The past can't be changed and must be accepted. Your only decision is what behavior is necessary to move forward.

Anger, once it takes hold, requires a certain amount of time to subside. As you practice anger management techniques, the amount of time necessary will decrease substantially. Ideally, you want to reprogram yourself to eliminate the anger stage completely.

Anger can be managed, controlled, and eliminated. Anger is a habit that develops over time. Modifying any habit takes desire and effort. The more determined you are to change, the more rapid the results will be.

Living without anger will make you happier, healthier, and more pleasant to be around. You will accomplish more with far less stress and frustration.

40. Interacting With Difficult People

Everyone has to interact with difficult people. No matter what you do or where you go, there is no escaping these troublesome individuals. Usually these people are not specifically targeting you, but treat everyone with the same disdain. Perhaps you can relate to one or more of the following examples.

You call your credit card company to correct a billing problem and the person taking your call is abrupt and rude. She treats you as if you are an annoyance rather than a valued customer.

Your boss gives you an urgent task instructing you to drop everything else to complete it. The next day he reprimands you for not completing your other work. Attempting to explain that you were just doing what was requested is of no help.

Someone you supervise always has an excuse for why they consistently arrive late. Regardless of what you say, he insists he is a victim of circumstances and bears no responsibility.

133

You have trouble getting an insurance claim resolved. Although you have always paid your premiums on time, the company appears to be utilizing every available strategy to delay or avoid payment.

You call a government office and it's impossible to find a person who can help you. Each person you are transferred to claims they are unable to help and instead directs you to someone else.

When encountering a difficult person, there's no way of knowing what's happening in their life or what kind of day they have had. You come along and become the target for their frustrations.

You don't have the time or energy to waste getting sidetracked by someone's attitude problem. Keep your goal in mind. What are you trying to accomplish?

If you allow yourself to get personally offended by their actions several things will happen. You will be diverted from your objective. You will become engaged in a battle that serves no purpose. You will become frustrated and annoyed.

The other person has a problem and you don't want their problem to become yours. You don't need to rehabilitate, accuse, blame, punish, condemn, or engage in a fight. Don't succumb to the temptation to react in the same manner in which you are treated.

Don't make it an issue of pride, dignity, or image. A feeling of "I don't have to take that" will not be productive. You want to solve your problem, not sway a jury. Don't become angry or indignant. You don't want to burn bridges or say things that you will regret.

Be polite, pleasant, firm, insistent, persistent, and consistent. You want to control the situation and guide it to a satisfactory resolution. Always take the high road. A nasty retort on your part, regardless of how justified it may be, won't serve you and will not be forgotten by the other person.

Treat people with a smile. Say please and thank you. Make your point with questions rather than statements. Saying things like "Can you please help me?," "I need your help," or "If you can't help me can you switch me to someone who can?" will often be surprisingly productive.

If the person you need to speak with is unavailable, calling back is less frustrating and more effective than leaving messages and waiting. Call back as often as necessary to resolve your problem. Persistence is the key to being the squeaky wheel that gets oiled.

With a difficult boss, ask for clarification if you are unsure what is expected. Ask which task has the highest priority. Send a memo or email confirming your understanding. If you are later criticized for not completing the other tasks ask, "Didn't you request that I complete the most important task first?"

If you are continually having trouble with an employee, threatening or warning them hasn't worked. Lead people with questions. Everyone needs to understand that they are responsible for the results of their behavior. Ask the individual how they would solve the problem if they were in your shoes. It's much more effective when a person thinks an appropriate solution is their idea rather than having it imposed on them.

Having a good attitude and taking the proper approach makes interacting with difficult people much more productive.

41. Dealing With Conflict

One of my reader's, Mary, was having a problem with her mother-in-law, Janice (names have been changed). Janice constantly said things that infuriated Mary. She criticized and questioned everything Mary did.

Mary would become defensive in response and attempt to explain or justify her actions to Janice. Janice always seemed to know what Mary was most sensitive about and focused on those areas.

Mary was very frustrated. Her stomach knotted up whenever she had to see or talk with Janice. Mary wanted to know how to apply the principles and concepts presented in this column to her situation.

Dealing with conflict from those closest to you, such as relatives, spouses, or friends is a difficult challenge. These people know you the best and understand what your sensitivities are. When their intent is less than benevolent, they seem to excel at getting under your skin and are a constant source of agony.

No one can control your emotions without your participation. You can't control what other people say, think, or do but you do have total control over how you respond. When someone intentionally acts in a manner intended to set you off, you don't have to take the bait.

If your actions or beliefs are questioned, you are not obligated to explain or defend yourself. Do so if you want to, not because you have to. When a person doesn't agree with what you are doing, you probably won't change their mind no matter how hard you try. Disagreeing with, or giving them a piece of your mind only identifies your sensitivities without deterring their behavior. There are people who will exploit your sensitivities just to cause you anguish.

What can you do when someone's words or actions annoy you? You can confront them about their behavior. If they are benevolent and considerate and their actions were inadvertent, they will likely apologize and refrain from repeating the offensive behavior.

Other people have malicious intentions and are looking to aggravate you. They seem to always know exactly what upsets you. An effective way of dealing with this type of person is to avoid reacting.

Refrain from arguing or objecting to their offensive behavior. Just smile and don't respond. At first this isn't easy because they make your blood boil. When they eventually realize you no longer react, they will often leave you alone and look for easier prey.

You are not going to get these types of people to change who they are. You have probably already tried unsuccessfully. When feasible, minimize your interaction with people who seek conflict. Removing yourself is not conceding; it's prudent behavior that preserves your peace of mind.

No one can irritate you, annoy you, or take advantage of you without your permission. When you stop reacting to someone's actions they will get frustrated and may try even harder to egg you on. But as you hold your ground and refuse to be drawn in, their behavior will subside. Even if it doesn't, you will have conditioned yourself not to react, so it won't matter anyway.

42. Staying Sane in an Insane World

The world appears as if it's going crazy. Terrorism, new diseases, scandals, crime, and abuses comprise daily headlines. We're awash in bad news. Wherever you look, you're bombarded with details of what's wrong with the world.

It's very easy to become overwhelmed, overcome, and disheartened by current events. Everything looks as though it's in chaos and makes no sense. A feeling of helplessness is not uncommon.

Although there is seemingly much that is out of your hands, there are numerous circumstances you can manage. How do you stay positive instead of being frustrated? By concentrating your energy on those situations within your influence.

How can you do this? Make a list of all things that you affect. Write down who and what brings you joy and pleasure. Itemize everything you have a positive influence over. Consider all aspects of your life: family, friends, acquaintances, colleagues, and community.

Don't overlook the little things. What might seem insignificant to you may mean a lot to others. Train yourself to become more aware of those special moments that happen spontaneously and often go unnoticed.

Post your list and read it daily. Repetitive concentration on the items you noted will help displace the daily onslaught of negative news. The more you expend your energy on the good, the less you are distracted by the bad.

The big world is simply a combination of everyone's individual worlds. If people stayed focused on making their own world the best it could be, the big picture would improve as well. Spend your time influencing what you can rather than worrying about what someone else should be doing.

Brighten someone else's day by making them smile, making them happy, or helping them, and you improve your own disposition. How you feel impacts those you come into contact with. Smile and people will smile back. If you're depressed, you can make others depressed. One of the simplest ways of elevating your mood is by boosting someone else's.

Treat others with respect. Be courteous and polite to everyone you come into contact with. Try to help other people whenever possible. Say "please" and "thank you." Simple considerate actions produce wonderful results. For example, surprise someone by letting them in front of you in a checkout line when shopping.

Human nature is what it is and hasn't changed much since the beginning of time. There will invariably be numerous imperfections that you are not happy with. It's part of life.

If you don't recognize and accept this fact, you are destined to a life of frustration.

Become involved in your community. Don't allow your representatives to function without knowing how you feel. Make your opinions known. At the very least you will be an active participant rather than a spectator.

Limit your exposure to negative news and events depicted on TV, radio, and in print. Continually discussing depressing topics with others will depress you. It's one thing to stay informed and another to be obsessed.

Spend time with those you care about. Keep your life balanced between work and play. Engage in activities that make you and others happy. Avoid destructive behavior. Don't take your frustrations out on those you come into contact with.

If you spend time on those things that are within your control, you are much more likely to feel positive and stay sane.

43. Be Happy - Have Fun

Are you happy? Do you have fun? Do you look forward to and enjoy each day? If so, great. If not, why not? Each person has his or her own interpretation of happiness, fun, and enjoyment. All outlooks are valid as long as the well being of others is not compromised by your pursuits.

Happiness is not synonymous with selfishness. Life is not a sentence, it is an adventure which should be enjoyed and savored. No one is trapped in any particular situation. Everyone has options and choices. The direction of your life is up to you.

What can you do if you're not happy with your current circumstances? If you're unhappy, you must understand why before you can plan a strategy to correct it. Are your feelings of discontent associated with work or your personal life?

If you are unhappy with your work, what is the problem? Do you like your occupation but would rather work for someone else or yourself? Maybe you don't like the hours you work. Perhaps you'd rather be doing something different entirely.

BRYAN GOLDEN

The time and effort expended to get where you are in your line of work is not a reason to stay there. You're never locked or trapped into a particular situation. Although it takes effort to change, it requires more effort to suffer. Possibly you completed college or a training program and now realize that you hate what you are doing. Should you stay in a career that makes you miserable until you retire because that's what you went to school for? If you do, you sacrifice many years of happiness that would be yours if you were engaged in work you really enjoyed.

If you could choose any occupation, what would it be? There's no limit to the ways you can earn a living. Whatever you do for recreation, others are earning a living from it. If you need additional knowledge or training, it's readily available. You will never be as young as you are today, so get in gear and start working toward what you want! Don't waste another moment suffering in misery. Start today to be proactive in your quest for happiness.

What about discontent with your personal life? Are you discontent with any of your relationships. Does your spouse, partner, boyfriend, or girlfriend understand how you feel? In any relationship, the other person is an integral part of your existence. Your partner may not be aware of or understand your frustrations.

What to you is obvious may not be evident to the other person. Relationship issues are often directly linked to communication problems. When all those involved in a relationship make a concerted effort to understand the feelings of each other, problems can often be solved. If each person strives to sincerely listen and communicate, an environment that nurtures happiness is created.

144

You and your partner may be incompatible. If you have exhausted all options and just can't make a relationship work, what do you do? Making choices in this case is not easy, but no one benefits when everyone is miserable. Remaining unhappy may seem to be a path of least resistance but carries a steep price.

Perhaps you're unattached but want to be in a relationship. Seek out activities where you can meet other people with a similar mindset. The more people you encounter, the better the chances of finding that right person for you. Be creative. The potential for meeting someone is virtually unlimited. School, clubs, organizations, and vacations are some of the many settings where people connect.

How do people become unhappy? Usually the progression is gradual. If changes were sudden and drastic, no one would accept a loss of joy. Each small change or event taken by itself is often treated as no big deal. So, bit by bit, you adjust and learn to live with it.

But the cumulative effect has a drastic impact. Unhappiness sneaks up on you, and before you know it, you feel trapped. Avoid settling for that which doesn't work for you. Pay attention to warning signs, gut feelings, and intuition. Don't ignore the small stuff. Things overlooked can snowball and drain you of joy and happiness.

If you are happy and having fun, you will get the most out of life and set a good example for others.

44. Don't Worry

There's never a shortage of things to worry about. You can worry about what has happened or will happen, what you did or didn't do, what someone else did or didn't do, what someone will or won't do, or what others will think. At times, the mind tends to run rampant conjuring up scenarios to stress over.

More than ninety percent of what people worry about never materializes. Worry drains time and energy without producing any positive results. Worry is like being in a rocking chair; it's a lot of activity that doesn't get you anywhere. There's a big difference between worry and action. Worry won't accomplish anything whereas positive action can improve circumstances and achieve much.

A common syndrome is paralysis by analysis. This occurs when a person becomes stuck vacillating between different options due to worry about the most prudent path to take. The result is no action being taken. Watch a squirrel darting back and forth in the middle of the road as a car approaches and you'll see this phenomenon in action. Unless the squirrel makes a decision to run off the road, he'll be a squirrel no more.

Ironically, worry attracts the very things you don't want. Your thoughts are a magnet. Whether good or bad, you tend to attract those situations you focus on. When you worry you are dwelling on an undesirable outcome. Thinking about what you do want and how to attain it is a powerful antidote for worry.

Worry and stress are interrelated. If you are worrying, you are stressed. Worry can undermine your health. Numerous physical ailments including high blood pressure, ulcers, headaches, aches, and pains have been linked to stress and worry.

A recent study found that stress changes the chemistry of the blood. Levels of Interleukin-6 (IL-6) sharply increased in stressed people. Ailments such as heart disease, arthritis, osteoporosis, type-2 diabetes, and certain cancers have been associated with elevated amounts of IL-6.

The study also found that people tend to respond to stress behaviorally by engaging in activities that increase the level of IL-6. For example, under stress people may overeat and/or smoke. IL-6 is secreted by fat cells and smoking increases its concentration.

Additionally, stress adversely affects sleep and can reduce the amount of exercise people engage in. Normal sleep regulates the levels of IL-6 and exercise reduces it.

So how do you stop worrying? First and foremost, you must develop an awareness of when you start worrying and what you are worrying about. Many people are so used to worrying that it has developed into an automatic response that is accepted as a normal emotion.

Once you begin identifying when and about what you worry, you can start training yourself to stop worrying. Don't confuse not worrying with a displacement activity. A displacement activity is a distraction that simply masks the worry. Worry that is pushed below the surface will fester, grow and increase in intensity. For example, when worrying, a person may get lost in organizing and cleaning their home. This activity displaces the worry without effectively diffusing it.

Worry can be broken down into one of three categories; worry about the past, the present, or the future. Worry about the past is completely pointless. The past is over, it can't be changed. Period. End of discussion.

Steps can be taken to alleviate worry about the present or future. First, ask yourself what is the worst that can happen? Second, prepare to accept the worst if you have to. This is not to be cruel, but to enable you to proceed to the third step. If you don't take this second step, you can become immobilized with fear and worry. You are then unable to identify options or take action that would actually make a difference.

Third, calmly take positive action to improve on the worst case scenario. Action is the only remedy for worry. Taking action means taking control of your life rather than feeling and acting like a victim.

Even in instances where you have no direct control over what you are worrying about, you do have the ability to formulate alternative plans of action in response to various scenarios playing out.

You are either a master over worry or worry will control and, at the very least, drain you.

45. Managing Stress

Do you ever feel stressed? Is stress a regular component of your lifestyle? What exactly is stress? What causes it and what can you do to manage and reduce it?

What you experience as stress is the result of your reaction to the events, circumstances, and people you encounter. The more you feel frustrated, a victim, helpless, a target, or picked on, the more you feel stressed.

You are surrounded by potential sources of stress. Your job, family, friends, schedule, traffic, and finances are among the many possible origins of stress you are exposed to on a daily basis.

Managing stress is accomplished by monitoring and regulating your reaction to situations and circumstances. If your response is a knot in your stomach, tension, or anger you are in the grip of stress. You don't have to become stressed when faced with stressful situations.

Stress affects you mentally and physically. Mental manifestations include irritability, sleeplessness, a lack of focus, emotional swings, a feeling of helplessness, and a short temper. Physical symptoms include elevated blood pressure, ulcers, headaches, weight gain, and aches and pains.

Don't underestimate the destructive effects of stress. The consequences can be debilitating. Left unchecked, stress can cut years from your life span and severely undermine your quality of life.

Our innate fight or flight response is responsible for physiological symptoms. Our bodies are designed to run from or combat any perceived source of stress. Modern society, however, prohibits our doing either. Stress therefore finds an outlet by affecting us mentally and physically.

If you attempt to manage stress by trying to control your environment, you will only succeed in exacerbating your stress level. You can't change people or circumstances but you do have control over yourself. The only effective strategy for controlling and reducing stress is learning how to manage your reaction to your environment.

Unless and until you change the way you react to stress, you will keep experiencing the same symptoms. You can't run away. Wherever you go, you will find stress inducing situations. Only by reprogramming your internal stress handling mechanism will you free yourself from the clutches of stress.

An effective method for managing your stress is constructing a written stress management handbook. Identify and write down everything you stress over. Next detail your reaction to each of the sources of stress. The handbook is your own private document, so be honest in your self-assessment. Different people have varying reactions to the same circumstances. You are only concerned with your behavior.

For each of your reactions, describe an alternate response that would minimize anxiety. For example, if obnoxious people stress you, your ideal reaction might be to ignore them without getting upset. Whenever you find yourself feeling stressed, recall and be guided by your alternate response.

Written identification of the causes and effects enables you to formulate a stress management strategy. The following are some additional effective techniques for reducing stress.

Take responsibility for your life. Don't blame others. You are the only one with the power to change things. Strive to effectively communicate your feelings and desires. Others don't know how you feel or what you think unless you tell them. Don't take the actions of others personally. If you are kind and considerate and someone treats you poorly, it's because they have a problem.

You don't want to allow frustrations and anger to build up internally. Emotional suppression is destructive. Doing so substantially elevates stress levels. You need to restructure how you interpret and react to sources of stress.

Managing and reducing your stress level improves your health and enriches your life.

46. A Healthy Body

Living happy and healthy requires that you pay attention to your physical and mental state. You are an integrated system of mind and body. To stay healthy both require use, exercise, and challenge. This chapter will focus on the body and the next one will concentrate on the mind.

Your physical condition has a tremendous impact on your mental state. Maintaining a healthy and active body enables you to feel good. Your body provides your brain with blood, oxygen, and nutrition. Proper diet and exercise enhances your health. The food you eat is the fuel used to power your body. Just as a car won't run correctly if there are contaminants in the gas, your functioning will be impaired by poor nourishment.

Everyone is subjected to stress daily. In the past, there were physical threats that literally threatened one's survival. Historically, the human body reacted to such danger with either fight or flight. Today, most of the stress you experience is mental. Yet your body still wants to react by running or fighting. When you encounter stress but running or combat is not an option, the stress is internalized.

Evidence indicates that bottled up stress can cause or contribute to a multitude of physiological malfunctions including diseases, aches and pains. Exercise, at the very least, is an outlet for stress. If you were to fight or run, you would be giving stress a physical outlet. Exercise provides the same outlet, but in a more culturally accepted manor. Even without stress, adequate exercise is essential for the proper functioning of your body.

Everyone has different physical abilities and limitations. Surprisingly, people with no physical limitations take their body for granted much more than those who have some type of restriction. You must work with, and get the most out of, what you do have. Regardless of your situation, there is much you can do to get exercise.

Your body is comprised of muscles that require activity to stay healthy. Without use, your body deteriorates. Exercise is not an all or nothing proposition and can easily be incorporated into your normal activities. You don't have to train to be an Olympic athlete.

Walking, one of the best exercises, can be done regularly, virtually anytime and anywhere. When driving to work or the mall, park as far away from the entrance as you can. Take stairs instead of elevators or escalators. During lunch, eat light and spend part of the time walking. There are numerous books and videos available that demonstrate many exercises that can be performed at home without any special equipment.

The type of exercise you engage in is not as important as consistency. Select a form of exercise that you can and will do regularly. Doing a little every day is much more effective than doing a lot every once and a while.

There are numerous philosophies on nutrition and diet. People have different metabolisms and what works well for one person may not necessarily work for you. If you're not happy with the way your body feels, examine what and how much you eat.

Most people eat more than necessary to maintain proper bodily functions. Overeating can lead to weight gain, lethargy, depression, as well as a host of physical problems. Adjusting how much you eat is one of the simplest things you can do, although not necessarily the easiest.

If you want to eat less, don't try to drastically cut back in one day. Determine your ultimate goal, then work towards it by reducing how much you eat five percent at a time. Once you get used to each cutback, drop another five percent. Repeat this process until you reach your goal. The amount of time it takes to achieve your goal doesn't matter. What's important is that you steadfastly stick to your plan.

Take care of your body and it will take care of you. Feeling healthy will enhance everything you do.

47. Take Chances

The following was written by an 85-year-old woman:

If I had my life to live over, I'd dare to make more mistakes next time. I'd relax; I'd limber up. I would be sillier than I have been this trip. I would take fewer things seriously. I would take more chances.

I would climb more mountains and swim more rivers. I would eat more ice cream and less beans. I would perhaps have more actual troubles, but I'd have fewer imaginary ones.

You see, I'm one of those people who lived sensibly and sanely hour after hour, day after day. Oh, I had my moments, and if I had to do it over again, I'd have more of them. In fact, I'd try to have nothing else.

Just moments, one after the other, instead of living so many years ahead of each day. I've been one of those persons who never goes anywhere without a thermometer, a hot water bottle, a raincoat, and a parachute. If I had it to do over again, I would travel lighter than I have.

If I had my life to live over again, I would start barefoot earlier in the spring and stay that way later in the fall. I would go to more dances; I would ride more merry-go-rounds. I would pick more daisies. - *Nadine Stair*

People develop a comfort zone where they feel life is safe, secure, and consistent. When a child is growing up, they are not afraid to take chances and try new things. Exploration is the key to their education. Children will attempt anything. To them, the world is an endless source of fascination and wonder.

All of mankind's accomplishments have been attained by individuals who have taken chances to explore that which was not yet known or understood. Throughout history, those people who have accomplished the most are those who have been willing to take the most chances.

Columbus, Louis and Clark, the Wright Brothers, Thomas Edison, Dr. Jonas Salk, and Edmund Hillary are just a few examples of people who have left their comfort zone to learn and achieve. They ventured into the unknown without any guarantee of success. Had they chosen a safe and secure path, today's world would be radically different.

With age, we develop an aversion to taking chances. We are afraid of losing what we already have. Fear of the unknown and the prospect of failure have a paralyzing effect. Subsequently, people lose sight of the fact that life has unlimited potential. To tap into that potential, you have to continually reach out for it.

When we stop taking chances, we stop growing and learning. The tradeoff for perceived safety is stagnation. Life is not a practice run. If you don't strive for what you want now, when will you? Each new day is a journey into the unknown. People feel secure when they don't take chances. However, it's a false sense of security and doesn't guarantee safety. What it does is limit one's potential.

Taking chances is not synonymous with being reckless or impulsive. Taking chances entails doing things where the outcome isn't assured. This can be done with intelligence and planning. It entails doing research, assessing the benefits and risks, and then moving out into the unfamiliar.

Babe Ruth wouldn't have set the records he did were he afraid of striking out. In addition to setting a record for hits, he also set a record for strikeouts. Why be jealous of what others accomplish? There is nothing special about them. They are just willing to strike out more than others.

Live in a manner where you won't have to look back and say, "I should have taken more risks." Learn from Nadine and others who have a lifetime of experience behind them. Venture out from your comfort zone. Take chances. Partake of life's infinite potential.

BRYAN GOLDEN

So where do you go from here?

Change doesn't happen overnight, but you can begin to change immediately. Everyone's life has room for improvement and growth. Now that you have read this book, you've been exposed to many concepts that have had a potent impact on millions of people.

You can make any changes you want. Look in the mirror and meet the person responsible for you. No one else can change you and you can't change others. Everything you need you already possess. This book helps you to find, uncover, and cultivate it. With determination, you can become and accomplish anything.

Repetition is the key to learning and transformation. Pick one principle most important to you and focus on it. Reread the applicable chapters regularly. Ideally, read at least one each day.

Strive to make one small change daily. At times, you may feel frustrated or discouraged. Don't give up, keep going, and stay on track. Accelerate your progress by sharing these ideas with others. The more you give, the more you receive.

158

Once you feel one change has taken hold, move onto another and repeat the process. Self-development is a lifetime endeavor. As you evolve, new horizons, potential, and goals appear.

You can live your life any way you choose. Don't procrastinate, start now. You are about to embark on a wondrous adventure with unlimited rewards.

BRYAN GOLDEN

About the Author

In 1983, Bryan founded his management consulting firm. Starting from scratch, he had far more enthusiasm and drive than knowledge or experience. Utilizing all of the concepts contained in this book, Bryan was able to quickly develop a successful enterprise. He has applied these principles to helping his clients enhance and expand their businesses. Bryan is also a highly rated adjunct professor, motivational speaker, author, and syndicated columnist. His popular column is enthusiastically read by a nationwide audience.

Bryan's column, *Dare to Live Without Limits,* is carried by various publications and distributed throughout the country. He consults with businesses of all types and sizes. Bryan is also available to give a presentation to your group or meeting.

This book is ideal for distribution throughout corporations and organizations. It also makes a great gift. Volume discounts are available.

Please contact Bryan for more information on any of the above.

You are invited to write to Bryan with your experiences applying the concepts in this book or with any questions or comments you may have.

The author may be contacted at info@BryanGolden.com or visit his web site www.BryanGolden.com.

Write to the author at

Bryan Golden
c/o Power Point Press
Beekman Road
Hopewell Jct., NY 12533

CPSIA information can be obtained
at www.ICGtesting.com
Printed in the USA
FFOW02n2321170116
20353FF

9 780975 368800